A JOURNEY OF RICHES

Building your Dreams

11 stories to inspire you into action

Published by Motion Media International
Editing: Gwendolyn Parker, Chris Drabenstott and Donna Barclay
Cover Design: Motion Media International
Typesetting & Assembly: Motion Media International Printing: Amazon and Ingram Sparks

Creator: John Spender - Primary Author
Title: *A Journey Of Riches - Building your Dreams*
ISBN Digital: 978-1-925919-11-0
ISBN Print: 978-1-925919-12-7
Subjects: Self-Help, Motivation/Inspiration and Spirituality.

Acknowledgments

Reading and writing is a gift that very few give to themselves. It is such a powerful way to reflect and gain closure from the past; reading and writing is a therapeutic process. The experience raises one's self-esteem, confidence, and awareness of self.

I learned this when I created the first book in the *A Journey Of Riches* series, which is now one of nineteen books with over 200 different co-authors from forty different countries. It's not easy to write about your personal experiences and I honor and respect every one of the authors who have collaborated in the series thus far.

For many of the authors, English is their second language, which is a significant achievement in itself. In creating this anthology of short stories, I have been touched by the amount of generosity, gratitude, and shared energy that this experience has given everyone.

The inspiration for *A Journey of Riches, Building your Dreams* came from my own experience of settling for less than I truly deserved. Of course, I could not have created this book without the eleven other co-authors who all said YES when I asked them to share their insights and wisdom. Just like each chapter in this book makes for inspiring reading, each story represents one chapter in the life of each of the authors, with the chief aim of having you, the reader, living a more inspired life.

I want to thank all the authors for entrusting me with their unique memories, encounters, and wisdom. Thank you for sharing and opening the door to your soul so that others may learn from your experience. May the readers gain confidence from your successes, and also wisdom, from your failures.

I say thank you to my family. I know you are proud of me, seeing how far I have come from that 10-year-old boy who was learning how to read and write at a basic level. Big shout out to my Mom, Robert, Dad, Merril, my brother Adam and his daughter Krystal; my sister Hollie, her partner Brian, my nephew Charlie and niece, Heidi, thank you for your support. Also, kudos to my grandparents, Gran and Pop, who are alive and well, and Ma and Pa, who now rest in peace. They accept me just the way I am with all my travels and adventures around the world.

Thanks to all the team at Motion Media International; you have done an excellent job at editing and collating this book. It was a pleasure working with you on this successful project, and I thank you for your patience in dealing with the various changes and adjustments along the way.

Thank you, the reader, for having the courage to look at your life and how you can improve your future in a fast and rapidly changing world.

And I'd enjoy connecting with readers, as I love sharing stories. You can email me here: jrspender7@ gmail.com

Thank you again to my fellow co-authors: Dr. Colleen Sabol-Olitsky, Tony Gunn, Lyn Croker, Beth Lydia Ranchez, Dario Cucci, Leon Beaton, Lynette Gehrmann, Cindy Vazquez, Narelle Burgess and Jennifer Kumar.

I hope you have enjoyed this co-authored experience as much as I have.

With gratitude

John Spender

Praise for
A Journey of Riches book series

"The *A Journey of Riches* book series is a great collection of inspiring short stories that will leave you wanting more!"

~ Alex Hoffmann, Network Marketing Guru.

"If you are looking for an inspiring read to get you through any change, this is it!! This book is comprised of many gripping perspectives from a collection of successful international authors with a tone of wisdom to share."

~ Theera Phetmalaigul, Entrepreneur/Investor.

"*A Journey of Riches* is an empowering series that implements two simple words in overcoming life's struggles.

By diving into the meaning of the words "problem" and "challenge," you will find yourself motivated to believe in the triumph of perseverance. With many different authors from all around the world coming together to share various stories of life's trials, you will find yourself drenched in encouragement to push through even the darkest of battles.

The stories are heartfelt personal shares of moving through and transforming challenges into rich life experiences.

The book will move, touch and inspire your spirit to face and overcome any of life's adversities. It is a truly inspirational read. Thank you for being the kind open soul you are, John!!"

~ Casey Plouffe, Seven Figure Network Marketer.

"A must-read for anyone facing major changes or challenges in life right now. This book will give you the courage to move through any struggle with confidence, grace, and ease."

~ Jo-Anne Irwin - Transformational Coach and Best Selling Author.

"I have enjoyed the *Journey of Riches* book series. Each person's story is written from the heart, and everyone's journey is different. We all have a story to tell, and John Spender does an amazing job of finding authors, and combining their stories into uplifting books."

~ Liz Misner Palmer, Foreign Service Officer.

"A timely read as I'm facing a few challenges right now. I like the various insights from the different authors. This book will inspire you to move through any challenge or change that you are experiencing."

~ David Ostrand, Business Owner.

"I've known John Spender for a while now, and I was blessed with an opportunity to be in book four in the series. I know that you will enjoy this new journey like the rest of the books in the series. The collection of stories will assist you with making changes, dealing with challenges, and seeing that transformation is possible for your life."

~ Charlie O' Shea, Entrepreneur.

"*A Journey of Riches* series will draw you in and help you dig deep into your soul. Every author has an unbelievable life story of purpose inside of them. John Spender is dedicated to bringing peace, love, and adventure to the world of his readers! Dive into this series, and you will be transformed!!"

~ Jeana Matichak, Author of *Finding Peace*.

"Awesome! Truly inspirational! It is amazing what the human spirit can achieve and overcome! Highly recommended!!"

~ Fabrice Beliard, Australian Business Coach and Best Selling Author.

"*A Journey of Riches* Series is a must-read. It is an empowering collection of inspirational and moving stories full of courage, strength, and heart. Bringing peace and awareness to those lucky enough to read to assist and inspire them on their life journey."

~ Gemma Castiglia, Avalon Healing, Best Selling Author.

"The *A Journey of Riches* book series is an inspirational collection of books that will empower you to take on any challenge or change in life."

~ Kay Newton, Midlife Stress Buster, and Best Selling Author.

"*A Journey of Riches* book series is an inspiring collection of stories, sharing many different ideas and perspectives on how to overcome challenges, deal with change and to make empowering choices in your life. Open the book anywhere and let your mood choose where you need to read. Buy one of the books today; you'll be glad that you did!"

~ Trish Rock, Modern Day Intuitive, Bestselling Author, Speaker, Psychic & Holistic Coach.

"*A Journey of Riches* is another inspiring read. The authors are from all over the world, and each has a unique perspective to share, that will have you thinking differently about your current circumstances in life. An insightful read!"

~ Alexandria Calamel, Success Coach
and Best Selling Author.

"The *A Journey of Riches* book series is a collection of real-life stories, which are truly inspiring and give you the confidence that no matter what you are dealing with in your life, that there is a light at the end of the tunnel, and a very bright one at that. Totally empowering!"

~ John Abbott, Freedom Entrepreneur.

"An amazing collection of true stories from individuals who have overcome great changes and who have transformed their lives and used their experience to uplift, inspire and support others."

~ Carol Williams, Author-Speaker-Coach.

"You can empower yourself from the power within this book that can help awaken the sleeping giant within you. John has a purpose in life to bring inspiring people together to share their wisdom for the benefit of all who venture deep into this book series. If you are looking for inspiration to be someone special, this book can be your guide."

~ Bill Bilwani, Renowned Melbourne Restaurateur.

"In the *A Journey Of Riches* series, you will catch the impulse to step up, reconsider and settle for only the very best for yourself and those around you. Penned from the heart and with an unflinching drive to make a difference for the good of all, *A Journey Of Riches* series is a must-read."

~ Steve Coleman, author of *Decisions, Decisions! How to Make the Right One Every Time.*

"If you want to be on top of your game? *A Journey of Riches* is a must-read with breakthrough insights that will help you do just that!"

~ Christopher Chen, Entrepreneur.

"In *A Journey of Riches*, you will find the insight, resources, and tools you need to transform your life. By reading the author's stories, you, too, can be inspired to achieve your greatest accomplishments and what is truly possible for you. Reading this book activates your true potential for transforming your life way beyond what you think is possible. Read it and learn how you, too, can have a magical life."

~ Elaine Mc Guinness, Bestselling Author of *Unleash Your Authentic Self!*

"If you are looking for an inspiring read, look no further than the *A Journey Of Riches* book series. The books are an inspiring collection of short stories that will encourage you to embrace life even more. I highly recommend you read one of the books today!"

~ Kara Dono, Doula, Healer and Best Selling Author.

"*A Journey of Riches* series is a must-read for anyone seeking to enrich their own lives and gain wisdom through the wonderful stories of personal empowerment & triumphs over life's challenges. I've given several copies to my family, friends, and clients to inspire and support them to step into their greatness. I highly recommend that you read these books, savoring the many 'aha's' and tools you will discover inside."

~ Michele Cempaka, Hypnotherapist,
Shaman, Transformational Coach & Reiki Master.

"If you are looking for an inspirational read, look no further than the *A Journey Of Riches* book series. The books are an inspiring and educational collection of short stories from the author's soul that will encourage you to embrace life even more. I've even given them to my clients too so that their journeys inspire them in life for wealth, health and everything else in between. I recommend you make it a priority to read one of the books today!"

~ Goro Gupta, Chief Education Officer,
Mortgage Terminator, Property Mentor.

"The *A Journey Of Riches* book series is filled with real-life short stories of heartfelt tribulations turned into uplifting, self-transformation by the power of the human spirit to overcome adversity. The journeys captured in these books will encourage you to embrace life in a whole new way. I highly recommend reading this inspiring anthology series."

~ Chris Drabenstott,
Best Selling Author, and Editor.

"There is so much motivational power in the *A Journey of Riches* series!! Each book is a compilation of inspiring, real-life stories by several different authors, which makes the journey feel more relatable and success more attainable. If you are looking for something to move you forward, you'll find it in one (or all) of these books."

~ Cary MacArthur, Personal Empowerment Coach

"I've been fortunate to write with John Spender and now, I call him a friend. *A Journey of Riches* book series features real stories that have inspired me and will inspire you. John has a passion for finding amazing people from all over the world, giving the series a global perspective on relevant subject matters."

~ Mike Campbell, Fat Guy Diary, LLC

"The *A Journey of Riches* series is the reflection of beautiful souls who have discovered the fire within. Each story takes you inside the truth of what truly matters in life. While reading these stories, my heart space expanded to understand that our most significant contribution in this lifetime is to give and receive love. May you also feel inspired as you read this book."

~ Katie Neubaum, Author of *Transformation Calling*.

"*A Journey of Riches* is an inspiring testament that love and gratitude are the secret ingredients to living a happy and fulfilling life. This series is sure to inspire and bless your life in a big way. Truly an inspirational read that is written and created by real people, sharing real-life stories about the power and courage of the human spirit."

~ Jen Valadez, Emotional Intuitive and
Best Selling Author

Table of Contents

Preface

I created this book and chose this collection of authors to share their experience about how they developed their courage. This is to assist you and raise your belief that you too can overcome your challenges and move one step closer to fulfilling your dreams and live life on your terms.

Like all of us, each author has a unique story and insight to share with you. It just might be the case that one or more of these authors have lived through an experience that is similar to circumstances in your life right now. Their words could be just the words you need to read to help you through your challenges and motivate you to continue on your journey.

Storytelling has been the way humankind has communicated ideas and learning throughout our civilization. While we have become more sophisticated with technology, and living in the modern world is more convenient, there is still much discontent and dissatisfaction with one's reality. Many people have also moved away from reading books, and they are missing out on valuable information that can help them to move forward in life with a positive outlook.

I think it is essential to turn off the T.V.; to slow down and to read, reflect, and take the time to appreciate everything you have in life.

I like anthology books because they carry many different perspectives and insights on a singular topic. I find that sometimes when I'm reading books that has just one author, I gain an understanding of their viewpoint and writing style very quickly, and the reading becomes predictable. With this book, and all of the books in the *A Journey of Riches* book series, you have many different writing styles and viewpoints that will help shape your perspective towards your current set of circumstances.

Anthology books are also great because you can start from any chapter and gain valuable insight or a nugget of wisdom without the feeling that you have missed something from the earlier episodes.

I love reading many different types of personal development books because learning and personal growth is vital to me. If you are not learning and growing; well, you're staying the same. Everything in the universe is growing, expanding, and changing. If we are not open to different ideas and different ways of thinking and being, then we can become close-minded.

The concept of this book series is to open you up to different ways of perceiving your reality and to give you hope. It is to encourage you and give you many avenues of thinking about the same subject. My wish for you is to feel empowered to make a decision that will best suit you in moving forward with your life. As Albert Einstein said, **"We cannot solve problems with the same level of thinking that created them."**

With Einstein's words in mind, let your mood pick a chapter in the book, or read from the beginning to the end and allow yourself to be guided to find the answers you seek.

With gratitude,

John Spender

"Start where you are.
Use what you have.
Do what you can."

~ Arthur Ashe

CHAPTER ONE

An Abundance of Dreams

By John Spender

Build Your Own Dream

Powering through the water with ease, feet kicking
with force, arms gliding across the surface faster than
I had ever experienced — left, right, left-right, I sped
across the pool. I knew I was a long way in front. After
my third tumble turn, I could see that I was at least four
body lengths in front of the next swimmer. I touched
the wall at one minute and three seconds. Although this
was a long way off from Alexander Popov's 100-meter
freestyle short course world record of 46.74 seconds, I
had only been consistently training five days a week for
three months. I was 18 at the time, and a little old to start
competitive swimming, but the coach elevated me to the
senior elite training squad. It was a bit daunting to turn
up to training with the likes of Brett Hawke, a five-time
Australian National Champion, Glen Housman, an Olympic Silver Medalist, Steven Dewick, an Olympic Bronze
Medalist, and a lot of other talented swimmers. I continued to show up, as I wanted to make my dad proud of me.

> **"If you don't build your dream, someone will
> hire you to build theirs."**
> ~ Tony Gaskin

My only goal was to develop a stronger bond with my father, who loved swimming and was a competitive swim-

mer in the adult swim squads. My parents divorced when I was five; it was a confusing time in my life. Many young children grow up without their fathers, and only able to see them a dozen times or so weekends in a typical year. Being the type of person who can see the positive in a negative situation, it turned out not to be the most fulfilling dream, simply because swimming brought my dad alive much more than it did me. I was living and pursuing his dream and not my own. Hours upon hours of training for one moment of exhilaration on race day (if you're lucky)... no thanks; not for this rooster. I learned a timeless lesson about building dreams: make sure they're aligned with your values and not someone else's, no matter how noble the cause. Parents have ideals and dreams for their children, believing that if they would only live into the vision they have for them, somehow, they'll be alright. Fulfilling your parents' vision for your life is how you discover what you don't want to do with your time.

Living the Dream

Earlier on in life, I was terrified to go after the dreams in my heart for fear of not being good enough. I remember having a conversation with my Uncle Alex on my grandparents' farm. I was in year eleven when Alex asked me what I wanted to do after high school. I told him that I wanted to be a marine biologist, but I didn't think I could get a good enough grade. He stopped me mid-sentence and explained that, "John, you can do anything in this life if you believe it is possible. It doesn't matter if no one in your family has ever been to university before. With determination and a positive attitude, you can achieve anything in your life." If you don't feel like you deserve what you desire, it doesn't matter what you do; it'll always elude you. I never made it as a marine biologist, mostly because the subjects I needed to get good grades in had nothing to do with marine mammals, sea life, or the ocean, for that matter. In incubating a dream, you need to be able to touch it! Experiencing the dream through a vision board is a great place to start, but you need to do more than visualize your dream in your mind. I'm talking about actually living into the dream. In high school, we had "work experience," where you'd go and work in your field of interest for a week or two. Now, there wasn't anything available in the area of marine biology, but I did get a week of work experience at the Australian Reptile Park on the Central Coast of NSW. I did enjoy the work, but it was mostly feeding and cleaning up after the animals. I handled some of the pythons and alligators, but mostly, it was cleaning up their mess, and the pay wasn't the best either. Needless to say, I sidestepped that career move.

You can imagine how hard it can be to know if a dream is genuinely right for you until you have touched it. You need to match your vibration and belief with your dream. It's the best way to squash the doubt, overcome the fear, and increase your certainty that you deserve the very thing that you want. It's near impossible to get into vibrational harmony when you are fulfilling someone else's dream. Sure, you can have success through hard work and grinding, but your heart isn't in it and you feel empty inside. Touching the dream first gives you an experience of it and you also can see if this is the reality you really want to manifest. Another example of touching the dream would be that you have always wanted to own a farm, but you don't know how it's going to happen. You need to touch the dream; so, of course, you would go to a real estate agent in your ideal area and walk on the farmland, pondering the benefits of each property that you see, and then make a ridiculously low offer you can afford. This is how Richard Branson bought Necker Island in the British Virgin Islands in the Caribbean in his early days of starting Virgin Records before he became a billionaire. Richard and his girlfriend, Joanne (now his wife), decided they would pretend to buy this island for the free flight to inspect the property. After walking around, they really wanted to own the uninhabited island but couldn't afford the five million dollar price tag, so he made the estate agent an offer of $100,000, and they were quickly flown back to the mainland.

> **"Sail away from the safe harbor.**
> **Catch the trade winds in your sails.**
> **Explore. Dream. Discover."**
> ~ Mark Twain

On returning to the UK, Branson increased his offer to $180,000. It turned out that Scottish billionaire, Lord Cobham, needed short-term cash, and he finally accepted the offer of $180,000. Branson, only 28 at the time, wanted to entertain rock stars on the island. The next challenge was the government wanted him to build a resort on the island in three years, or it would return back to the state. Branson had only founded Virgin Records six years prior to the purchase of Necker. Scrambling for cash to save the island, he invested ten million dollars in three years to build his famous luxury resort. Today, you can rent the island for around 80,000 dollars a night, all-inclusive, for thirty people. I love that story! It's almost like Richard was treating the entire process as a game, taking it seriously but not too seriously. Stepping into the dream doubles your vibration of belief; you're forced to face any fear that may be blocking you, and you get to feel what it's like to diminish the fear of the unknown and feel what it would be like to live your dream.

When A Dream Finds You

What I'm about to share with you might sound strange with all that I've been saying about dreams, but I've never really been a goal-orientated person — not in the sense of having a list of short-term, medium-range, and long-term goals. I find that it places you under too much pressure. People can forget to live a life that makes them happy. Instead, you can get caught up charging through life from one goal to the next without stopping to smell the roses. Like a donkey chasing a carrot on a string at the end of a stick, avoiding a whack on the ass from the stick but never quite reaching the carrot... It's easy to oscillate between pleasure and pain, rather than standing in love, manifesting and allowing the dream to unfold through inspired action.

The first real dream of mine actually found me. I was just about to complete year 11, going through the motions at school, feeling uninspired, while trying to get a greens keeper's apprenticeship but getting nowhere. Out of the blue, my aunt told me about a horticulture program and sent me a bunch of information in the mail. I filled out the application form and prayed I would be accepted. In a nutshell, the program was years 11 and 12, but with only math, English, and geography, the rest of the course included horticultural subjects with one day of hands-on work per week. I thought, 'Are you kidding me? I get to study a topic that interests me, and in doing so, I gain employment afterward?' Although I would have to repeat year 11, at least I didn't have to waste another year studying subjects that I had no interest in learning. I wanted to be the best I could be. Feeling motivated, I excelled at topping the class in almost all my subjects. I went from a C grade student to an A grade student because I was studying subjects that were of interest to me. It was a dream that I wanted to evolve into, and growing my commitment became second nature. The school system I was in made me feel inadequate and looked upon me as a failure or a student that wasn't capable of excelling in academic subjects.

"The secret of getting ahead is getting started."
~ Mark Twain

After a few years, I owned a landscaping company with 15 staff, developing large council contracts in the eastern suburbs of Sydney. We even won a paving contract at Darling Harbor for the Sydney Olympic games. I never set out to create my own business. My aunty talked about it a few times with me, but I never thought it would happen so soon. After two years of working full-time, my mom helped me to buy my first pickup and to place an ad in the local paper in Sydney. I was away, never looking back. I already had several contacts, and recommendations were following in. It wasn't like I focused on starting a business, but life just unfolded that way. I think you do need to be intentional about what you are focusing on, though. I was dialed into learning about horticulture as much as I could be. I discovered you could expand who you are with the right point of focus, and I applied that knowledge to my life. My dedication brought me a college degree in horticulture, parks and gardens, landscaping, and landscape design. Not learning how to read and write in the English language until I was nine was an advantage, as I discovered the gifts of determination, dedication, depending on myself, and taking responsibility for my life at an early age.

Tackling Your Dream

Chasing dreams doesn't work for me; you need to become the dream. I found that I must get intentional on what I want to breathe life into, and immerse myself in going through the motions, step by step. Where you can become stuck is to worry about how or what the next step should be rather than placing all of your energy into taking the action you know is next. Doing this gets you in flow with what you are creating, and that's when the next step becomes apparent. That's a big one for people to grasp. It's so easy to get caught in stagnancy, and before you know it, you've become best buddies with procrastination. It's the most natural path because our brains aren't wired for us to be fulfilled and happy. Guess what the brain is wired to do? Keep us alive! It seems like an excellent ideal, right? Running a pattern of procrastination is better than being dead. There have been several studies that conclude that the fastest way to break the habit of procrastination is to forgive yourself. That's right — forgiveness is the key. By going easy on yourself and giving yourself a break, researchers found that people can reduce the amount of procrastination that they experience. The opposite, of course, is to put yourself down, and tell everybody about it, highlighting how it's causing a big problem in your life. You know when a person is in that loop, they are going to get more of what they don't want for a while.

"If you believe it'll work out, you'll see opportunities.
If you believe it won't, you will see obstacles."
~ Dr. Wayne W. Dyer

Once you've given yourself some slack and completed the forgiveness process, then you'll want to generate some wins by starting small. When I write a chapter for this book series, I break the goal of writing an entire chapter into easily-manageable steps. The task appears less daunting that way, making it easy to catch the wind in your sails, gaining momentum. Clarity is indeed the gateway to empowerment, opening the door to creating energy in your writing; and before long, your story will begin to write you. Even after the 18 plus books, I have produced over the last four years. The initial writing process is still a little slow. To encourage myself to get going, I set a target of just writing for 30 minutes. I play sacral chakra Tibetan singing bowls by Sonic Yogi; his recording is tuned into the frequency of the second chakra, the energy center of creativity. The beats lay the foundation to get into the right mental state to create. The recording is relaxing, easy to listen to for 30 minutes as you begin to build momentum with your writing practice. You want to make the writing process as easy as possible. To paraphrase Tim Ferris, "Give yourself permission to write some crap, to begin with; you can always come back later and refine what you wrote." The most important point of focus is to begin; start where you are and focus on 'progress over perfection.'

It's been a dream of mine to write and share my knowledge and journey with the world. I didn't set out to create the *A Journey of Riches* book series. My attention was on helping others bring their inspirational stories to the world, but after the success of the first book, I had people asking when I was going to do another one. I hesitated because of the amount of time, energy, and effort that goes into collating a book, especially an anthology with many different authors. My goal now is to create 101 books in the series. That seems like a lofty target to achieve, so I have to focus on just one book at a time. If you are mindful of helping other people and supporting them to get what they want, then you'll naturally get what you want. I believe that obsession comes with a price; the fixation on one goal means that you are always saying no to anything that isn't the dream. I see a balanced life between a multitude of interests as healthy and necessary to living a life full of zest and freedom. Say no to an average life so that you can say yes to an extraordinary one.

Preparing for Your Dream

Without your health, it's hard to enjoy any dream that comes to fruition. I recently had a wake-up call regarding my health. I had been living the laptop lifestyle for over six years, but I wasn't exercising regularly. Also, being a "sweet-tooth," I was consuming way too many desserts. The books have been selling and doing well. The movie I wrote and am producing has been gaining momentum. But amid my success, I was recently diagnosed as pre-diabetic. I had poor blood circulation; I was getting feelings of pins and needles in my hands and feet. Managing my emotions also became a struggle with many high-highs and low-lows. It was apparent that I needed to make some changes to my lifestyle.

Slowly, I began reducing the amount of sugar intake and increasing my exercise routine to a daily one. Yoga became a big part of my life and I now go four to five times a week. If I'm not doing yoga, I'm going on long walks or hiking waterfalls around Bali. I also do Freeletics; I use an app called 7 Minute Workout, which is a series of push-ups, jumping jacks, lunges, squats, sit-ups, and various other bodyweight exercises. This helps me to stay in shape, keep my blood sugar levels in check and strong enough to manifest perfect health. Another turning point was being introduced to an incredible Balinese healer who helped me to empower my body to heal itself, improving my circulation and blood flow. He also helped me remove my childhood trauma from my body, where it was stored in various organs, especially in my stomach. My health got worse before it got better because all the issues were coming to the surface. I experienced intense acid reflux, stomach pains, extreme bouts of belching, and even diarrhea.

"Every human being is the author of his own health or disease."
~ Buddha

My healer had me go to purification ceremonies every new and full moon. At the new moon, I would go to the beach with a Balinese offering that consists of a banana leaf, various kinds of flowers incense and seawater. I would pray for perfect health and drink a baby green coconut. I do a similar routine for the full moon. However, I would go to a water temple in the regency of Bangli called Sudamala with natural water fountains flowing out of a cliff face.

Praying at the various fountains, and immersing yourself in them; giving an offering and praying for perfect health at each one. There are around fourteen of these fountains. In the end, a Balinese priest will be waiting to give you a water blessing. He or she will splash water on your head three times with a water brush, then you sip the water three times, and lastly, you wash your face three times. You take dry rice, and place some on your third eye, in-between your eyebrows, and place some on your throat chakra.

It takes commitment to heal your body; I'll do anything natural to enhance my health, especially if someone with certainty believes it'll make a difference. You want to be healthy when you realize your dreams, so you can live into them and enjoy your new reality. You have to put yourself in a position to be in alignment with your dream. For example, I can't dream successfully of being an Olympic Gold Medalist if I'm not doing all the training with a coach. Moving into perfect health has been my way of aligning with my dream of launching an impactful personal development film that inspires three million people or more around the world. I'm going to be in great shape and healthy when it occurs. I've already noticed a huge difference with my energy; my mood swings aren't as dramatic and my circulation has improved; no more pins and needles in my hands and feet. The weekly healing massages have also sped up my recovery, as well. It's been slow going at times, but no matter how I feel, I show up and take the necessary action steps.

For me, that's making sure I exercise every day, eating lots of fruits, vegetables, and drinking plenty of water and fresh juices; doing intermittent fasting, and once a year, doing one juice or coconut water fast. It also entails maintaining a healthy lifestyle and the necessity of this can go right over your head if you haven't had a health scare in your life. It's until something you enjoy is taken away that you truly value it.

I'm a firm believer that we shape our reality with our thoughts and actions that we continue to live every day. In Louise Hay's groundbreaking book *You Can Heal Your Life*, she shares a list of diseases and the probable emotional cause of the various illnesses. The emotional challenge associated with diabetes is a yearning for what might have been — in my case, allowing my past traumas to dictate how I show up today. Louise also mentions a need to control your experience, a sense of deep sorrow and no sweetness left. In the past, I've tended to isolate myself from friends, spending time alone in nature to focus on my dreams. Our bodies can communicate with us, pointing out where we need to make adjustments in our lives. Grinding for long hours day after day doesn't work for my body or social life anymore and so I've had to prepare for my dreams differently. My minor health scared has highlighted the necessity to be prepared to live my dream when it comes to fruition and to live with joy in the moment.

Making Room for Your Dreams

You may have heard of the sad story of a circus elephant that was caught in a fire and burnt to death. The strange thing was the elephant's leg was tied to a stake in the ground. Being fully grown, the elephant could have pulled the stake out of the earth and ran to safety. The elephant trainer later explained that when the circus elephants are young, they are chained around the back leg to a pole in the ground, and the baby elephants can't break free. No matter how hard they try, they aren't strong enough, and they eventually stop trying. The elephants become so conditioned that when they are fully grown, the keepers can place a rope around their foot and the elephant won't even try to break free. Conditioning and beliefs are two significant hurdles you face in making your dreams a reality. It's powerful to be able to look back and reflect on your past experiences. You can then decide on what changes you would like to make in your life and not be bound by your conditioning. We all need to break the habits of our comfort zones, if we want to have the courage to fulfill our own dreams.

There have been numerous elephants burnt in circus fires over the years. The one that springs to mind is The Ringling Brothers circus fire at Cleveland in 1942. The menagerie circus tent caught alight, and due to the highly-flammable waterproof coating on the canvas, the flames spread quickly. It was waterproofed with the traditional mixture of paraffin and white gasoline. The fired lasted all but 20 minutes, but with the straw lying around everywhere and a breeze blowing from the nearby lake, the blaze was swift. Luckily, no one was hurt. However, the damage to the animals was horrendous. As you can imagine, all the animals were in a panic; only the elephants remained stationary. Being trained and conditioned, the half dozen elephants would only move on command. Walter McClain had a fierce reputation as a master trainer, being a genius of the craft. Fortunately, he was one of the first to the scene, immediately taking command of the small herd of elephants.

Entering the rapidly incinerating tent with his men, the team scurried behind the elephants removing the back stakes from the rear legs of the gentle giants. Then on McClain's command, the elephants pulled the front stakes out with their trunks. Another order from McClain and they marched out in procession, trunk to tail. Dripping pieces of the tent had burned the majestic beasts, the flesh hanging off their bodies, peeling off like flaking paint, but they moved to safety.

This was a horrific disaster. It makes me think about people I know who don't have their shit together, living the same life day in and day out, unwilling to make the necessary changes to reach their full potential and live their dream life. It can be as easy as deciding to yank the stake out of the ground and claim your dreams. We are strong enough to overcome any obstacle in our way; otherwise, we wouldn't be given the challenge in the first place, right? The question remains, are you willing to let go of your past conditioning to bring your ideal reality into existence? You can't do both and expect to be successful in your endeavors. Sadly, so many dreams go up in smoke before they are realized; badly bruised and burnt, most people settle for average after their first failure.

"Our greatest dreams are never out of reach, only out of belief."
~ Dr. Wayne Dyer

The rescuers, after moving the small herd of elephants out of the burning flames, couldn't reach three remaining elephants. One, Ringling Rosie, was freed from her chains, but she was scared frozen, unable to leave the burning tent. The heat was overbearing, forcing the men out. McClain stayed the longest, burning the side of his face. From the outside, patrons watched Ringling Rosie stomping back and forth as the flames engulfed her. The final death toll was four elephants, including Ringling Rosie, thirteen camels, nine zebras, five lions, two tigers, two giraffes, two wildebeest, two white fallow deer, two Ceylon donkeys, one axis deer, one puma, one chimpanzee, and one ostrich. The Cleveland circus fire is a tragic story that awakens within me the motivation to not let my music die inside while I'm still alive.

I can't tell you how many times I've been frozen into inaction — not from a blazing fire, but from fear of achieving my greatest potential. The vision is there; the next step is there, but so is avoidance and stagnancy. Remember, that's the time to build yourself up to touch the dream, revisit your vision board, call your friends and ask them about your strengths, and immerse yourself in studying your craft from past greats. Take small, consistent action steps, anything to build momentum towards your dream. This will help break the shackles of your past conditioning and limiting beliefs. Step by step celebrating the small wins along the way, any dream can be realized. As long as you have your health, you can do anything. Above everything else, health is number one. I'm working on living in the present moment, letting go of past programs, to find joy in the now and rediscover the sweetness of each day. Building someone else's dream isn't ideal, but failing to create your own dream is a crime whose penalty is going to your grave with your unlived dream buried with you.

"Too many of us are not living our dreams because we are living our fears."

~ Les brown

CHAPTER TWO

Your Money Mindset

By Dr. Colleen Olitsky

"Prosperity is not an outward possession, rather an inward realization."
~ James Allen, As a Man Thinketh

For the Love of Money

My kids are only eleven and eight, and they already know how much I love money. Here's how I know: when my dad visited from Philadelphia, they asked him, "What were the first words Mommy spoke when she was little?" He answered, "Money." He was joking, of course, because my whole family knows that I had always loved money, even when I was young. But for most of my life, that love of money had come from a sense of hoarding and a mentality of lack, not from the mindset of abundance I enjoy today. I'm excited to walk you through my journey from scarcity to abundance and share pearls of wisdom that will hopefully impact your money mindset. My desire is to inspire and motivate you to take responsibility for your attitude and beliefs about money as you begin to read and learn more about how to improve them.

What is a Money Mindset?

What is a money mindset and why does it matter? Most people think of money as coins and pieces of paper, but money is also energy. So many emotions, both positive and negative, have a presence in our money. Most people never realize how their thoughts and feelings about money either help or hurt their chances at accumulating more of it. Money is not the enemy; rather, it has the potential to bring you happiness and peace. Shifting your relationship with money can help you change all aspects of your life because no matter how much money you have or make, it is *your* inner perceptions about money that determine your true wealth. If you have an unhealthy attitude toward money, no amount will change the negative feelings you might harbor about it. As my Dad teased, from as early as I can remember, I've had a strong desire to be wealthy, but I had a poor mindset. I never had any sense of peace or security about money — only stress, no matter how much money I made — and I knew I had to make a change and set foot on a path toward building a positive money mindset.

Money Isn't Everything

Let me stop here and interject that people have different definitions of success. My definition includes being happy, healthy, wealthy, and in love. Being financially wealthy is only one piece of the big picture, but it's an essential piece. That said, I understand that money isn't everything. Over the years, I've learned that we, as a family, were already rich. We were surrounded by abundance, and I committed to stop overlooking that fact. My husband and I had our health, our kids, and a steady income from work we loved. We created a healthy balance between home and work. We loved living at the beach and having time with our families and good friends. Life was good! But I can recall so many times throughout my life when I was stressed out about money that it clouded over everything I had to be grateful for in my reality. I always worried about every dollar spent.

> **"Prosperity is first a state of mind, and then it translates itself into reality."**
> ~ Ron Willingham, *The Inner Game of Selling*

My Money Mindset History

As a child, I loved to earn money selling candy or helping my elderly neighbor, Mrs. Butler, with her mail and chores. I would count my earnings and wrap the coins in the bank coin holders. I loved to watch the amount grow and grow in my piggy bank. Actually, it was a little plastic safe with a combination lock on the front. I was always a saver, rarely spending my money on spontaneous purchases. Where did this habit come from? Probably my dad, who was old-fashioned and also rarely spent money on himself. Or perhaps it came from watching my mom spend money frivolously and not wanting to be like that. I believe that it was a combination of both of my parents' attitudes that strongly influenced me.

But I also modeled a scarcity mindset from both of them, too. In fact, I was just visiting with my parents and I mentioned this chapter I am writing, and my dad asked if I remembered that he used to get horrible headaches when he had to spend money. I hadn't remembered that until he mentioned it but I can assure you it greatly impacted my beliefs around money and how it should be (or *not* be) spent! I do remember that they were always stressed about money and that they spent more than they should have and weren't focused on saving. For years, my father worked long, hard hours as an electrician, but as the years passed, they never seemed to ever feel 'good' about money. It's hard to watch the people you love work hard yet never get ahead. I feel the same way now with my team, and it's why I enjoy inspiring and educating them on their mindset and how to live a life by design, not by default.

Today, at age 69, my father has had five knee replacements — two on one leg, three on the other, and he is still in constant chronic pain. It's heart-breaking to watch him try to play sports with my son but can barely walk. What's worse is that he still wakes up at 4:30 am to work the physically demanding job as an electrician. Now, I can say with certainty that he loves what he does. I can still remember him telling me that if I love what I do, then I've got life licked. But wouldn't it be nice to have the CHOICE to continue to work (or work only part-time) because you enjoy it versus having to work because you don't have the money to retire? The big lesson here is that who we grow up with affects us more than people realize. The trick is turning inward, and through self-reflection, discovering why you think the way you do and learning how you can let go of negative thoughts and beliefs, and begin the process of improving your mindset without being critical or placing blame.

Another influence that helped shape my money mindset was dating a financial advisor in college. After he met with my parents who were in their mid-40s at the time, he told me they were in trouble financially, and I was shocked. My father woke up early and worked so hard all day...how could this be? They weren't saving toward retirement the way they should. Simply put, they were spending more than they were bringing in. This seems like common sense, but most Americans are crippled with debt and can't sleep at night because they are overspending and under-saving. I knew I never wanted to be in that position, so I opened my first investment account in my junior year of college and started saving $100/month.

All Grown Up

Fast forward to when I was 26 years old, I was engaged to my dental school sweetheart, Jason, and we had just moved to Florida to begin our life together. We signed a contract to work for a managed care company with a guaranteed salary, and I was ready to start earning and saving some big bucks and start feeling some relief around money! We had taken the Florida boards that summer and were waiting to hear the results so we could get to work. The results came in: Jason passed; I had failed! I couldn't believe it. I couldn't work as a dentist in Florida. The managed care company offered me a position as a dental assistant. It was quite brutal those 6-8 months, earning only $12/hour, yet still having to pay for my dental student loans and disability insurance. I wasn't quite making the big bucks I thought I would make. This, along with my poor mindset, made it even worse. I wouldn't spend money on anything, even necessities. For example, I would let a faucet leak or fence be broken because I didn't want to spend money to fix it. Jason was not used to living like that, so we would argue about how the money was or wasn't being spent. Looking back, it seems so silly, but I just couldn't shake that 'hold onto every dollar' mentality. Within the next few years, our income increased dramatically with me working as a dentist. I had retaken the boards and passed; but even though we got around a $75,000 pay increase, I still continued to live in lack, just wanting to save and invest it all. Yes, we should live below our means, but with my mindset of lack, I took this to the extreme. I was happy we were saving a lot of money now, but doing it the way I was going about it was continuing to cause so many fights between Jason and me. He was not a big spender, yet I kept him living way below his means and what he considered his deserved level. I had created a lot of needless stress between us. I wanted to feel better about money but just didn't know how. To be blunt, I hated spending money. I wanted to spend only on the must-haves and save the rest. That said, I was open to opportunity, as long as it meant we could potentially earn more.

Investing in Home Rentals

As I mentioned, after dental school, Jason and I had moved to Florida and we rented a home near the beach. A year later, we bought our first home. Six months later, we purchased a second home. We were influenced by Robert Kiyosaki's book, *Rich Dad, Poor Dad*, and wanted to invest in real estate and make money through home rentals. In the early 2000s, being high-earning professionals, we could get bank loans for no money down — a good thing, or so we thought. As we figured it, we would buy a house a year and rent it out. If we did that for ten years, then, in 30 years, all of our houses would be paid off. Hurrah! We'd have lots of passive income rolling in from our ten rental homes.

But the truth is, we knew nothing about renting houses. Our very first renter ended up being a scam artist, and we had to set the eviction process in motion. It was so stressful in terms of both the process as well as losing money from no rent being paid. It certainly left a bad taste in our mouths. We did not continue our real estate journey; instead, a year later, we moved into the more expensive of our two homes because we loved the neighborhood. Even though we could earn more in rent with that home, Jason helped me see that the move would be worthwhile; we'd enjoy life more in that home. I look back now and see this as an example of how well we could balance each other if we took the time to communicate, listen, and compromise. But back then, this decision pointed out a glaring difference in our upbringing and respective mindsets. Today, with a lot of personal growth and communication, we are in harmony and rarely argue about money or how it is spent. I simply cannot believe how much time and energy was wasted all of those years. That's why I want to help others so much. Life doesn't have to be so hard; it's probably so much better than what you're feeling right now. I love showing people how to live in gratitude and abundance, no matter what they earn or how much debt they are in. And we know that expressing that gratitude will bring more to be grateful for, instead of complaining and attracting more to complain about.

Smile Stylist — Our New Dental Office

After working in corporate dentistry those first 3-4 years after school, we decided to open our own office. We wanted to be our own boss and run the office our way. We had also heard that you could earn more working for yourself, so of course I was on board. With hard work, dedication, and a $600,000 loan for the build-out, we opened Smile Stylist in April, 2006. We did pretty well those first 18 months but owning and operating a business is taxing in itself; then add in those $14,000/month practice loans, and "Ouch!" — talk about stress! Then the recession of 2008 and 2009 hit, just two years after opening our dental office. Opening a scratch practice is hard enough but when you specialize in smile makeovers, and seemingly overnight everyone's discretionary income flow seemed to stop, we felt the full effect of it. We went through two years of barely getting by. We felt as if we were drowning. Running a dental practice is very expensive. Your overhead includes that large practice loan, rent, staff, dental supplies, office supplies, continuing education, lab bills, building insurance, disability insurance, workman's compensation, student loans, marketing costs, and more. Today, our overhead is nearly $80,000/month. Back then, as a smaller office, it was probably closer to $50,000/month. We had some months where we collected $70,000 and earned $20,000, but we also had months where we only collected $35,000 and lost $15,000. We had also just had our first child in 2008, who was colicky and cried for five months straight; it was just awful! Jason and I were constantly arguing, and life felt pretty dim. No one would have known this looking at us; we always kept a smiling face at the office and for friends, but inside, I was really struggling. As the economy started to improve, I began to read books on self-development. These two factors helped me come out of the depression I was feeling and I started to feel hope about our future. The lesson learned was that there will always be ups and downs; you just have to remember to breathe and be grateful for what is going right and actively work on your mindset, both personal, as well as your attitude toward money. That was just a season in our life — our winter — and that's ok. Accept it but know that as long as you vow to never quit and continue working toward your goals, spring will come.

A Career Change

All through my early and mid-30s, I continued to struggle mentally by hoarding money and feeling a fear of lack whenever we spent money. As I mentioned, I had started to improve by reading personal growth books and listening to my mentors' advice about success. I finally felt like I was moving in the right direction by growing my mindset and success habits. Our office had done well after the recession and continued to grow from 2010-2014. We had our second child in 2011, and she was a wonderful baby; things were feeling so much better! However, in 2014, when our kids were three and six, I started really resenting having to be at the dental office. I was missing the beautiful summer days and precious time with my babies. I hated the rushing back and forth doing school pick-ups and drop-offs. Being a dentist and owning and operating an office is very time-consuming and overwhelming, especially with the insurance headaches, managing staff, and dealing with the "crazy" patents. It was so stressful, trying to be the best mother, best wife, best dentist and business owner, as well as take care of myself. That summer, I had finally just had enough. I was angry and unhappy and taking it out on my family who didn't deserve it. I called an acquaintance to ask about her career. I'd followed her on Facebook and read her posts for the past year, and I was intrigued by what I saw. One post celebrated her most recent promotion and how she was earning between $400-500K/year. That caught my attention! During that time, I was craving more "me time" and knew the stress of being at the office was affecting me in a negative way. From the outside, it looked like I had it all but inside I was angry and struggling to hold it all together. So, in August 2014, I said yes to the opportunity of network marketing. I loved the idea of being able to work from home and be able to spend time at the beach, pool, and gym, and still able to help people, both physically and financially.

A New Dream Takes Shape

I went into the profession of dentistry because I wanted to help people. I thoroughly enjoyed what I did. More than drilling on teeth though, I liked doing the consults, talking with patients, and helping them understand the value of a new smile. As I began to learn more about Network Marketing and how I could have a huge impact on others' lives by helping them in a different way, I fell in love with the industry. I loved being able to not only help them become healthier physically, but also assisting them in learning to dream again and to feel fulfilled and prosperous. With that discovery, I fully committed and jumped right in! That's right. I quit my job as a dentist to begin a career as a Network Marketer.

Building Something I Love

The five most recent years of my life have been truly life-changing in so many ways. I finally felt happy with what I was doing — building a business for myself. Although Jason and I had built our Smile Stylist practice together, it was mostly *him;* I often felt like I didn't really belong. So, when I 'found my tribe' with the Network Marketing company, Isagenix, I felt completed in a sense. People at Isagenix focused on personal growth and lifting up others. I had started reading self-development books in 2005, but it wasn't until June of 2011, while reading Jack Canfield's *Success Principles,* that I began to actually apply what I was learning, which was *connecting thought to action!* As Napoleon Hill stated, "Do it now!"

"Connect thought to action!"
– Dr. Colleen Olitsky

In the years between 2013 and 2015, I committed to developing quarterly habits. I chose topics such as 'food matters', 'daily exercise', 'be nice (intentionally) to Jason', 'stretching', and of course, 'expanding my money mindset'. I spent three months reading 10-15 books about the energy of money, happiness and money, and growing wealth. And when I say read, that means I read a book once with my highlighter and a second time with a colored pen to underline passages that hit me. Then I'd go through it a third time to write down concepts and quotes in a notebook. Today, I have five notebooks filled with my thoughts and notes on about 50 books. I have read and re-read them so many times that the concepts have become a part of me. They're *who I am* as a person. The affirmations, quotes, and declarations in these books became my thoughts and beliefs and soon affected my actions.

Again, I think back to how much time and energy I wasted by stressing about every dollar spent compared with how much was coming in. Today, I am thankful for all of the wonderful books I've read and mentors I've had who shared their insightful suggestions with me. I give gratitude daily that I positively mastered my money mindset; otherwise, I would be one of those people who have money but are still never happy. It is not about the money; it's about mastering your mindset. I know that improving my mindset has led us to the prosperity and fulfillment in life we enjoy today.

Embark on Your Money Mindset Journey

"There is a science to getting rich, and it is an exact science, like algebra or arithmetic. There are certain laws which govern the process of acquiring riches, and once those laws are learned and obeyed by anyone, that person will get rich with mathematical certainty."
~Wallace D. Wattles

I've learned that money can make you feel dreadful, envious, fearful, guilty, regretful, and angry. Or it can also bring you confidence, peace of mind, and happiness. It's up to you! Are you willing to let go of some of your old ways of thinking to make room for new ones that lead to a positive money mindset? I encourage you to just take the first step! Just begin, and then take the next step, then the next. Stay consistent. Do one thing every day so you maintain your momentum and avoid the start, stop, start, stop that keeps you stuck. Here are seven steps to take as you move forward to create your dream life:

1. Drop old ways of thinking, including fear.

Doing this requires you to stimulate thoughts that will empower you to reach toward your vision of wealth. What you believe about money has everything to do with how much money you will make. More than that, changing your thinking will change your beliefs, which will improve your behaviors. Your philosophy affects your thoughts, which directs your actions, which creates your results, and ultimately determines your lifestyle. For me, affirmations became my truths as I continually talked to myself about who I wanted to become. I've learned that self-talk largely predicts your future. Either faith or fear drives all people. You can fear an event that hasn't happened or have faith that something positive will occur. Why not put your energy into your faith rather than fear?

"Faith is to believe what you do not see; the reward of this faith is to see what you believe."
~ Saint Augustine

2. Have a meaningful plan as well as a financial plan.

As you embark on this journey of developing a positive money mindset, I want you to realize that a *financial plan* without a *meaningful plan* leads to knowing all the money in the world doesn't buy happiness. Fulfillment and achievement are both critical. It's such a hard dichotomy, but being appreciative will attract even more to be grateful for in life. I want to wake up, do what I love to do, work out, take a walk in nature, spend time with family, donate to causes I believe in, travel the world, and continually look for ways to increase my net worth. What does your meaningful plan process look like for you?

3. Establish new habits and make them stick.

I love setting habits, giving myself 90 days to implement one new change into my lifestyle. Over five years, that adds up to 20 habits! Now, even if only half of them stick, that's still ten new habits moving toward success. I suggest you learn and maintain the habits of thrift, frugality, and saving. You can act rich after you become wealthy. Wealth is not the same as income. Wealth is what you accumulate, not what you spend. It is the result of a lifestyle of hard work, sacrifice, perseverance, planning, and self-discipline.

**"Good habits are the key to all success.
I will form good habits and become their slave."**
~ Og Mandino, *The Greatest Salesman in the World*

4. Live below your means.

Don't allow your income to define your budget; live below your means. Sacrifice high consumption today for financial independence tomorrow. Even high-income producers must live below their means if they intend to become financially free. Value freedom above instant gratification. Most importantly, do not let your spending increase when your income goes up. Instead, increase the amount of money you put into your investments.

5. Create multiple streams of income.

Be open to opportunities and take calculated risks. I suggest creating multiple streams of income to focus on increasing your net worth. This takes both an offensive approach (earn more, keep more, grow it more) and defensive approach (spend less). Be open to learning and opportunities. Real estate ended up not being what we were passionate about but diversifying with network marketing helps alleviate the stress off of our dental office, as well as allows for extra cash flow to invest in other ventures.

> **"If you are not fully, totally, and truly committed to creating wealth, chances are you won't."**
> ~T. Harv Eker, *Secrets of the Millionaire Mind*

6. Don't worry, be happy.

If you worry about the little things when you're broke, you'll continue to worry about the more significant things when you're wealthy. So, have faith and have fun! Don't waste time in fear or worrying. Happiness comes from being aware and appreciative of everything in your life. Be happy and satisfied right now. You have everything you need; be in the moment, and accept what was, what is, and what will be. When worrying about money has become a normal way of life, stop it by creating a plan and a stress-free, well-ordered financial life by decreasing debt, living below your means, and buying yourself greater peace of mind and security, which brings over-all happiness. It's ultimately about feeling the power and peace of mind, and knowing you're in control of your financial life. You'll gain a priceless serenity.

7. Use money as a tool for what matters most to you.

How you manage money is more important than how much you make. I get more satisfaction from accumulating wealth and giving than from simply consuming more. Having good health, a loving family, caring friends, and a career you enjoy can bring you happiness without the luxury items, and so does having a house filled with love while focusing on the simple pleasures of family and friendship. The amount of money you spend on food and entertainment might be easy to reduce, but first ask this question: Are the hours you spend eating, socializing, and doing activities the happiest parts of your day? If yes, then don't give them up! When it comes to purchases, buy things that add meaning to your life. Anything that doesn't spark joy is meant to go. Get rid of it — donate, sell, or give it away.

What does a rich life mean to you? Once you determine what that is with your new positive money mindset, then you'll use money to build that lifestyle. It comes down to being clear on what is meaningful to you, what aligns with your values. Work towards goals that are consistent with your values (on how you live every day, your kids, marriage, friends, health, happiness, fun, pleasure, hobbies, job/career, laughter, leisure time, travel, where you live, your home, creating memories, security, and stability). Then you can shift money you spend in less meaningful areas to things that matter.

"Spend less on stuff and more on life. You want to channel money into living, not just buying."
~ Dr. Colleen Olitsky

Money can bring comfort, happiness, freedom, and flexibility; but first, prioritize what you value most. For me, it's a healthy, happy family based on a stable love-centered marriage. May your journey bring you the meaning you want based on a positive money mindset.

Immediate Actions to Start You on Your Journey

Make a list of your current beliefs about money.

_____

_____

Write down the challenges you might face around changing your money mindset.

_____

_____

List what you value most in your current and future life.

_____

_____

Know your expenses. Avoiding them will not make them go away or improve.

_____

_____

Start saving today! Live on what is left.

Begin reading life-changing books today! Commit to even just ten pages every day! That adds up! Imagine reading 3,650 pages in one year — that could be 15 powerful books! I believe that will change your life! I've created a book list below to get you started.

My Favorite Declarations

If I want something to change on the outside/physical level, I must be willing to make the necessary inside/mental changes.

I focus on whatever it is I want to create more of, and I am grateful for what I already have.

I focus on money and prosperity flowing into my life.

I am reprogramming myself through repetition and positive emotion.

The external conditions of my life will always be related to my internal state.

Be content with who you are, instead what you have!

Nothing is static; the universe operates through dynamic exchange of giving and receiving. Give that which you want to receive.

Being generous is a sure way to be happy; be greedy and you'll be met with misery.

Memorize your affirmations until they become a part of your thinking and your life; they become habits.

Book List

Secrets of the Millionaire Mind, T. Harv Eker

The Success Principles, Jack Canfield

The Slight Edge, Jeff Olsen

The Science of Getting Rich, Wallace D. Wattles

The Four Agreements, Don Miguel Ruiz

The Traveler's Gift, Andy Andrews

Tuesdays With Morrie, Mitch Albom

As a Man Thinketh, James Allen

The Greatest Salesman in the World, Og Mandino

Stop Acting Rich...And Start Living Like a Real Millionaire, Thomas J. Stanley

Money and Happiness, Laura Rowley

Money Can Buy Happiness, MP Dunleavey

Think and Grow Rich, Napoleon Hill

You Were Born Rich, Bob Proctor

A Happy Pocket Full of Money, David Cameron Gikandi

The Answer, John Asseraf

Philosophy for Successful Living, Jim Rohn

Ask and it is Given, Esther and Jerry Hicks

21 Secrets of Self-made Millionaires, Brian Tracy

7 Strategies for Wealth and Happiness, Jim Rohn

Earth is Hiring, Peta Kelly

Excuse Me, Your Life is Waiting, Lynn Grabhorn

30 Lessons for Living, Karl Pillemer

Rich Dad, Poor Dad, Robert Kiyosaki

The Business of the 21st Century, Robert Kiyosaki

"Seek your power from within. Start building your dreams. You will see the voices on the outside breaking your dreams, suddenly disappear."

~ Rasik Chhetri

CHAPTER THREE

Despondence, Dreams, and Sanguinity

By Tony Gunn

What does it mean when people say that they're "living the dream?" How would you define it? Where do your thoughts go when you think of a dream life? Do you think about fame and fortune? Does your first thought go immediately towards the big house, the nice car, and the high-profile career? Perhaps your dream is more straightforward, like having a family, a modest home with the white picket fence, the sweet puppy, and undeniable religious faith. Perhaps living your dream is as simple as financial freedom and the ability to travel the world. However we choose to define "living the dream," one thing remains true: if you ask a hundred people the question, you'll get a hundred different answers. Each person is unique and has her/his own version of a dream life, so dream-chasing will inevitably vary from person to person.

There are no specific recipes that need to be followed to make our dreams come true, and we don't need to follow the same footprints of the person next to us. Many modern-day influencers have general guidelines and messages to convey, like, write your goals down, remain positive, work hard, and strike first when an opportunity presents itself. As a general rule, I'd say that's pretty good advice, wouldn't you agree? There's a popular quote that says, "Everything that you've ever wanted is on the other side of fear." What does this mean to you? What fears do you believe are holding you back from chasing the dreams you desire most? Many, or probably even most of us, fear failure and change. It's simple human nature. There's something about feeling comfortable that creates a safe space for our fears. The problem is, nothing grows in the comfort zone. Our souls desire to be stretched, expanded, and continuously recreated.

I want to share an unconventional story of dream chasing with you. It's a story built through hitting rock bottom, failure, suffering, adapting to circumstance, and befriending internal demons. A path where comfort is ripped away, where the struggle becomes comforting, where perseverance is a lifeline, and valor is involuntary. This is not your typical "how-to" story for the dream chasing faint of heart. This is more like, "The guide to positive thinking by the overly optimistic in the face of insurmountable probability," but I believe that might be too long for the chapter title, so we'll go with "Despondence, Dreams, and Sanguinity."

Hello, my name is Tony Gunn, and I'd like to take you on a journey with me. Together, we will transcend the negative into positive, heartbreak into unconditional love, suffering into gratitude and failure into dream-making — a place where coincidence becomes synchronicity, death creates life, and we find a connection in the web of a confusing and ever-changing life.

First, let's hop into the old time machine and head back to my childhood, a place of poverty, confusion, and depression, countered by discord, diffidence, and birse. My earliest childhood memories consist of shopping for clothes at secondhand stores, mixing powder and water to create milk, devotion to religion, household animosity, and verbal obloquy. Blend this all together and you have the recipe for one acrimonious teenager.

As a child, I dreamt of becoming a professional football (soccer) player. I felt like this was the only way to get out of my "swamp of sadness" and penniless living. If I could manage to earn an athletic scholarship, perhaps I could also attend a flourishing university, attain a degree, and create a prosperous life. So, day in and day out, I practiced football tirelessly. In doing so, I completely disregarded my scholastic responsibilities, which, as you may imagine, ended up being a colossal mistake. I ended up graduating 129 out of 132 from my bantam-sized high school with a 1.26 GPA. For those of you who may not understand what this means, it means that there weren't any Division 1 universities in the country that would be willing to accept me with those grades. My only remaining opportunity for continued education and athletics was to attend a junior college somewhere.

I ended up being accepted to a small school in Western Maryland, USA. After my first season of football, as a freshman, I was the seventh leading scorer in the nation for the JUCO division. My academics were acceptable, and I was feeling quite accomplished! A year went by, and I was chomping at the bit for the opportunity to exhibit my skills as a more dependable and tenacious sophomore. I was grateful to learn from my coach that many nationally-ranked Division 1 universities were now beginning to consider me, including the likes of #1 nationally-ranked University of Maryland. I excelled as a sophomore, scoring more goals, becoming a catalyst for more assists, and even participating in a regional JUCO all-star event. Rumors were that Maryland was keen to bring me on board to be a starter on an already amazing team! I was creating my dream!

Now, if you've been paying attention to my story so far, you would have already recognized that school classrooms are my Achilles heel, and yes, academics were about to take me down once again. My sophomore GPA had dropped below a 1.0, and I was placed on academic probation. I was no longer a highly-anticipated recruit; instead, I was turning out to be just another "coulda been." My frustration got the best of me, and I transferred out of my Junior College and began to attend a religious Mormon university. By transferring to an NAIA school, I could continue playing football without having to sit out a year due to academic probation. However, within two months, I was dismissed from this University for not abiding by the rigorous Mormon criteria, and I was forced to head back home.

I was ashamed of myself and resentful at the world, but only because I wasn't valiant enough to face the guy staring back at me in the mirror. I began acting out, regularly throwing parties, drinking heavily, and smoking weed daily. To compound the situation, I didn't care if I maintained a job, so dealing drugs became my main source of income.

One fateful night at the ripe old age of 20, I decided to do the horizontal polka with a girl I had known for a few years, but mainly through friends of friends' friendships. It was on this night of exploration that put me on a significantly contrasting life path. We conceived a child, out of wedlock, without an understanding of life, and without love for one another.

It was now time to give up my childish antics and join the workforce. I was by no means ready to be a father, unprepared in practically every way imaginable. Financially, I knew it was going to be a struggle. Emotionally, I knew this was going to be a challenge. And physically, I knew there would be sleepless nights and long days. This realization was frustrating for me because I knew that I was repeating the same childhood cycle that I wanted so badly to avoid. Abortion and adoption were never really a consideration. Religion made me believe that abortion wasn't an option and I wasn't selfless enough for adoption. Even if I couldn't offer my kid the best life financially, I was damn sure that no one could give her more love than I could. So, I put my head down and started working. However, without knowing, this was another wiggle on the web toward my growth in life and engineering. I started working in a machine shop where we manufactured precious metals and created jewelry from raw material melted down in an internal refining plant. My specific job was to operate a punch press. Don't know what this is? You're not alone — not many do. On a punch press, you put a flat piece of metal underneath a harder piece of circular-shaped metal, push two buttons to activate the hydraulic automation, and punch a hole into the flat piece of metal. As you're probably already thinking, this job sounds repetitive, dull, and monotonous. It was. But it also enabled me to buy baby diapers and provide much more desirable insurance. I began asking questions constantly, learning more about the industry, working overtime, and doing whatever it took to earn that extra 25-cent raise each year. I started to absorb knowledge from my colleagues who had been in the industry for decades; and within a short period, I understood how to program machines, order materials, and manage the overall operations of the business. By showing this motivation, I was promoted to many positions which included department manager, company improvement committees, and even product development teams.

As we all know, with growth, there must always be the swing of balance and experience. Life was about to offer me a set of trials that my ego wasn't quite ready to accept, and once again, my life derailed and swung right back out of balance.

I was driving home from work one day when I noticed a looming dark smoke coming from the direction of my home. I felt the worst had happened and sped up to see if my fears were indeed a reality. As I pulled into my driveway, the worst was proven true. Our family house had caught fire and there was no saving it. Everything was lost, but fortunately, no one was hurt. To this day, when I'm asked about what I miss most that burned up in the house fire, and my answer has always remained the same:"the photos." Couches, TV's, clothes, and even an entire house can be replaced, but before the invention of cell phones and the cloud, pictures were priceless.

To make matters even more complicated, my brother was found guilty of intentionally igniting the fire which caused the house to burn to the ground, and he was sentenced to a year in jail. It was hard to visit him there, but I went every week, and eventually, the state let him out. From there, it went from bad to worse. About a month after his release, he was diagnosed with schizophrenia, placed into a mental institution, and was utilized like a guinea pig for the medical industry.

Throughout the ongoing family complications, it was vital for me to keep my thoughts at work, focus on the positives in life, and try not to allow the hardships to become suffocating. To be fair, as for most of us, I believe this is easier said than done, and it didn't take long for the stress of my experiences to start breaking me down. Ulcers started growing in my stomach, which led to a lack of sleep, constant pain, and random nose bleeds. Over time, my body began to deteriorate, and I found myself in the hospital with a deadly case of viral pneumonia. I was literally on my deathbed, contemplating life...wondering what I had done wrong, why I was being tested so harshly, and questioning if I was going to survive this test. My lungs were somewhere between 75-90% full of fluid, and even the oxygen tank that was connected to me was having difficulty keeping me alive. I slipped in and out of consciousness several times and the doctors had almost given up on me.

At this point, the only thing that was going to keep me alive was my own desire to live. Otherwise, my curtain of life was coming to a close. None of the antibiotics were effective with this particular strain of pneumonia, so my only option was to take a "rubber ball" that the doctor had given me and physically beat my lungs to break up the fluid. If I could break up the fluid, then I would be able to cough it out and hope that it wouldn't reattach quicker than I could remove it. After painfully striking myself, for what seemed like days, the doctors began to see a positive change. The fluid in my lungs began to break up, and it felt like I was going to survive. After a little over a week in the hospital, I was released to go home, and I couldn't have been more grateful to lie in my bed and eventually get back to work. Eventually, I began playing soccer again, and for the first time in my life, I started paying better attention to my health. Having a second chance at life also gave me a renewed spirit at work. My programming, machining, and engineering skills became more focused and inspired.

At this point in my career, I was making good money but believed that my acquired skills deserved better pay. I needed to make a momentous business decision: stay with the company I loved or leave my comfort zone and seek out a new company where I could continue to grow.

As I lay in bed one night contemplating my choices, I received an unexpected phone call from the bishop of the church I was irregularly attending. The news couldn't have been worse, or had come at a worse time. I was told that one of my best childhood friends had been shot in the head by a police officer, rushed to the hospital and was in critical condition. I hopped in the car immediately and drove to the hospital as quickly as I could. Coincidentally, my friend's brother, Howie and I both arrived at the same time, rushing into a room full of mourning friends and family members. As we walked into his hospital room, we noticed that he still had a heartbeat, but from his shoulders up, he was wrapped in rags, protecting whatever damage was done underneath. Howie and I embraced each other. Filled with both sadness and anger, we were overcome with emotion. Only minutes later, our brother died right in front of us. We watched helplessly as his body convulsed and then became motionless. We stood there in tears, furious and broken.

Despair and sadness once again took over my outlook on life; however, as the pendulum of life and experience swings, where there is despair on one side, there is hope on the other.

I was sitting at work one day feeling sorry for myself when a colleague came up and asked how I was doing. Of course, my reply was both positive and negative, and my colleague could sense my sadness. He mentioned that he was a music producer and music has helped him to release pent-up emotions and transcend pain. He then asked me if I'd like to make a song to see if it might work for me. After some time, I gave in, and the producer gave me an instrumental song to write to get me into the flow.

To be totally honest, the song was terrible! But at the same time, it proved to be one of the most healing experiences of my life. To this day, I'm grateful this guy came into my life and opened me up to such expression. I ended up writing over 200 songs, creating five albums, and releasing many childhood and adult traumas that had built up for what I believe to be many lifetimes.

But back to the timeline of experience, learning, failure, and dream chasing...

Initially, after writing the first song, I wasn't instantly healed; however, it was a start. There would still be quite a while before the transition from pain to peace would happen. Due to this continued imbalance of sadness, my work began to suffer again, and I decided to quit without telling anyone. I moved in with my older brother in Northern Carolina, and tried to start all over. I only stayed with him for three months, but it was the perfect amount of time required to heal and move forward with my life. I decided to move back to Virginia to be closer with my daughter once again, and I jumped back into the workforce. Unfortunately, I hadn't prepared as adequately as I should have, and I found myself homeless and sleeping in my car. I was able to snag a good job in the same field of work, but it would take some time to build up enough savings to have a steady place to call home. A gym membership allowed for regular showers, which was especially warming on cold winter mornings. Also, I have always been blessed with amazing friends, so once word got out that I was sleeping in my car, several friends were kind enough to reach out and offer me a couch and a bed for as long as I needed.

It wasn't too long before I was back on my feet again, thriving at work and life. I was now in the world of woodworking and helped run a large machine shop. This company was relatively new and had nearly infinite room for growth. I went from machine operator to CAD manager to graphic designer to interior designer and right-hand man to the owner within a few short months. I was killing it!

However, the closer I got to the top, the less I really wanted to be there. The more time I spent with the owner, the more unethical business practices were revealed. After several instances of questionable morality, I ended up quitting that job and replacing it with a position in the world of steel machining. I was brought on to run the research and development department, which allowed me to be more creative, and it felt like a breath of fresh air. In addition to the continued business success and growth, love walked into my life and I instantly felt all the goodness in myself, mirrored by another.

It was love that helped me recognize everything else around me. And yes, in this circumstance, it was a woman who reflected the true meaning of love; however, love itself is the teacher and not an object. Love emphasizes gratitude, health, happiness, and courage. Love transcends anger to understanding, frustration to patience, and unawareness to compassion. Love appreciates all experiences. The "good" moments are even more beautiful, and the "bad" moments are more easily viewed as an opportunity to learn. Coincidence starts to become synchronicity...and once we start paying attention to synchronicity, we can manifest the life we've dreamed.

I began to create optimum working conditions instead of accepting the situations that were presented to me. I started intentionally manifesting the reality that best served my soul, instead of accepting a circumstance and learning to deal with it.

Four years after meeting the reflection of love, we were married. A few months later, she was pregnant. I was fired from my job and she was keeping us afloat as a server in the restaurant industry. In the past, this would have been a burden to carry and a struggle to deal with, but now, this was a sign for us to make a change. We both looked at each other and asked, "What do we love most about life?" The answer was simple for us. We love the ocean, warm weather, and each other. Without hesitation, without a place for ourselves, without a guaranteed job, and six months pregnant, we loaded up the truck and drove down to Florida. A family member was kind enough to loan us a bedroom for a couple of months while we saved up for our place.

I took on three interviews the day I arrived and was hired by all three. After much deliberation, I decided on the third one, which is where I still work to this day. This job has taken me to over 50 countries and has allowed for such unimaginable experiences that, as a child, I could've never dreamed of experiencing. While traveling, I started studying natural healing, herbs, and earth medicines in my free time. I spent quality time with herbalists, shamans, witch doctors, sages, and other masters of energy, meditation, and medicine. Soon after, I launched my first company, which focused on photography, creative arts, and herbal teas (with float tanks as a future endeavor). We now live oceanfront in south Florida, where our younger daughter is homeschooled and travels the world as a part of her studies.

Creating the life you want is as much about focus and dedication as it is about love and gratitude. Turning your dreams into reality is about living in the moment with an appreciation for every experience that comes your way.

If you noticed, the beginning of my journey had very little to do with focus. Completely unaware of being on any path, I was subconsciously creating a dream of mine to see the world. If I hadn't started from the ground floor of my first machining company, I would have skipped stages of my learning process. If my health hadn't failed me, I never would've gotten into natural healing and the deeper roots for the reasons behind energetic work and how every emotion manifests itself physically. If it weren't for living a simple childhood, I wouldn't have had the appreciation for growth. If it weren't for all the trials and tribulations, I would've never learned courage, strength, perseverance, and patience.

You see, even without having a set of goals to achieve, dreams were still manifesting. I was always on the path that was meant for me, even in my most ignorant and naïve of life stages.

For me, this life has been a test to find out how to learn and appreciate the continued scenarios presented from duality and the swing of the pendulum. They say that we will never know what a good apple tastes like if we've never eaten a bad apple. Under the same understanding, we may never feel the purity of love without diving into the darkness of our demons. We cannot understand pure joy without experiencing a taste of pain.

As we come full circle to the first paragraph of this story, we all have different dreams. We all have different paths of getting there. What may work for me may not work for you. The key is to be open to whatever comes into your life and to appreciate these gifts for being precisely what they are. Nothing more and nothing less.

As I write this, I'm sitting at a Buddhist monastery in the Himalayan Mountains and I realize that my dreams are quite different from the monk sitting beside me in prayer. While we are both connecting to the energies around us, connecting to love and gratitude, and manifesting the reality we want to create, we are doing so in drastically different ways…and we are creating drastically different dreams.

So, what is my advice for creating the life of your dreams? Look within, find out what brings your soul its highest appreciation, and learn to love every experience along the way. Make sure that the dream you're trying to create isn't a dream that society has told you that you're supposed to have. Make sure your dream honors your soul. Forcing my agenda or my will on a circumstance has never proven to be effective in the long run. Don't focus on money; instead, concentrate on abundance. Don't focus on marriage; instead, focus on self-love.

There will be times of despair; but ask yourself what you're supposed to learn from the experience. There will be times of doubt, but always remember, you are the creator of your life and you have all the power necessary to create the life you want. There will be times of fear, just remember that fear only exists in mind and by applying courage, your soul will honor you. One of the greatest gifts you can give yourself is the ability to see life from a higher perspective; and by higher, I don't mean enlightened (although that may not hurt). What I mean is living life from a bird's eye view. If you can step back from a situation and look at it from a broader perspective to see what can be learned from the experience, then you have received the true gift of wisdom.

We are free to choose!

Yes, believe it or not, you have that kind of power. You have the power to write your own story, to forge your path, to make life as awesome or as miserable as you'd like. Victims find victims; victors find victors. The truth is that for every person who has read this story, there will be a unique introspective worth dissecting. Some of you will gain a profound connection with these stories....a feeling of something you know to be true, but have only tasted intermittently throughout your life. You will seek me out and want to know more. You'll want to hear the story firsthand, to look in my eyes and see the experience, the truth, the connection. You'll want to express gratitude and love. You'll want to believe that I can guide you. You'll want to feel this same connection for yourself. And there will be questions, oh so many questions!

I'm not here to force anyone to feel one way or another, nor am I here to judge the process of learning. I'm merely here to love you for being exactly who you are right now, and to be grateful for each and every unique perspective — to understand and be patient with everyone's path of life, including my own. We cannot be teachers unless someone wants to be taught. We cannot be students unless we choose to learn. We cannot be angels until we've faced our demons.

Your life, your story, your perception, your reality, your happiness...your choice!

There is a love in you that transcends mortality. You are as powerful as you want to be. You are as fearless as you choose to be. You are as beautiful as you believe yourself to be. Do not let the world dictate who you are.

It's easy to get caught up in the rat race, in our day to day routines. We can be consumed by stress, fear, worry, and work. Around every corner, there's gluttony, greed, ambition, and power. Many of us have become jaded to life because of this misdirection. We can forget who we truly are. Our lives, in every way, are a reflection of how we feel on the inside. So, if I asked you to name everything you loved about life, how long would it take before you named yourself?

No matter who you are, where you live, how you've been living, what you've done wrong, and where you are in life…it is never too late to remember who you are. Loving yourself leads to loving others, which leads to a happier perspective, and leads to a grateful life. But it all starts from within.

There is nothing outside of you that will satisfy your soul like the love you give yourself — not money, not power, not even the love of someone else. Once you have accepted yourself, the darkest areas of your soul, the most delicate parts of forgiving, you'll find love reflected all around you!

For most of us, when we love a flower, we pick it from the ground so that we can show others the beauty that we've found. And it's so beautiful for a time. But what happens to that flower? Even when we put it into the water, feed it, and love it, it dies quicker than it should. We have removed it from its source of life. If you genuinely love a flower; if you genuinely love something, you let it be exactly as you found it. You let it grow and bloom and flourish without pretending to know better. You trust that their path is ideally placed for them.

What does the future hold for me? Well, I won't pretend to know. I don't even have a set plan of action. What I do believe is that whatever life has in store for me, I will love it with all my heart and have gratitude for living in this moment, in this life, in this body, in this reality.

"A dream is your creative vision for your life in the future."

~ Denis Waitley

CHAPTER FOUR

The Foundations of Pursuing your Dreams

By Lyn Croker

**"Dare to live the life you have dreamed
for yourself.
Go forward and make your dreams come true."**
~ Ralph Waldo Emerson

Introduction

Dreams... what does pursuing your dreams mean to you?

Does the idea of pursuing your dreams fill you with fear, doubt and anxiety, or does it fill you with excitement, confidence, and motivation?

Truth be told, achieving your dreams comes at a 'price.' That 'price' is different for everyone.

In the words of Walt Disney, **"All our dreams can come true if we have the courage to pursue them."**

Let me give you an example.

I always had the dream of competing in triathlons. For years I dreamed about competing. I knew I would do it one day. You know those dreams where we say "one day"? But I knew that if I didn't put plans in place and make the sacrifices necessary to make it happen, it would just be a dream - a wish.

To pursue my dream, I needed to take *action*.

The Universal Law of Action states, "we need to take action steps to what we want."

I set myself some goals. Goals that would help me realize the sacrifices that I had to make to bring my dream into reality, such as getting myself in the right mindset for success and eliminating the fears, doubts, and negative thoughts that continually crept into my head (more on that later).

In fulfilling these goals, it would undoubtedly be essential to commit to the hard, physical training that realizing my dream would involve. Each and every day, I would need to train for two to four hours. I would need to educate myself on the right type of diet that would be compatible with my rigorous physical training schedule.

Additionally, I would need to have a team behind me, consisting of people such as a training partner and a coach. I would need to have triathletes on my team who could share with me the lessons they had learned during their journeys. I'd have to make sure my family would be agreeable to the time I was taking away from being with them.

Moreover, I needed to get the right tools and equipment such as a good bicycle, the right running gear and the right swimming gear. I'd need to get enough sleep and factor-in adequate recovery time. All this, and travelling to compete in different venues necessitated that I find the funds to finance this dream. No sweat!

When I was aware of the sacrifices that I needed to make to turn my dream into reality, then it was full-steam ahead from there.

Because a dream without goals attached to it is just a wish.

Have you ever had a dream to do, have, or be something but it was so far away that it seemed impossible?

The type of dream that was so big you didn't even know where to start? Maybe you thought, "I don't deserve that" or "I'm not smart enough to do that." Perhaps it's just me that has all these negative thoughts!

I have pursued so many dreams over the years. Many I have achieved and I have more in the pipeline: some big, some small. So, when asked to write this chapter by my good friend, John Spender, it seemed like a natural thing to do. It's very close to my heart.

Some dreams have taken me years and years to achieve – decades, even; while others I have achieved reasonably quickly.

There is no time limit on achieving your dreams. What's important is that you are taking baby steps towards it. As Creighton Abrams said, **"How do you eat an elephant? One bite at a time."** So hopefully, my examples in this chapter and other authors in this book will show you that you can achieve your dreams if you have the necessary *foundations* in place. Those foundations are critical to your success. Hell, they're essential even to pursue your dreams.

Foundations

Now that you know that pursuing your dream takes sacrifice, the other critical foundation is *why* - why do you want to pursue your dream? There are a ton of authors that talk in more detail about this. Some of my favourites are Simon Sinek, Les Brown, Brendon Burchard. They all discuss your "why" and how, if it's not the right "why" then it won't motivate you to take action or to overcome the hurdles you will face on your journey.

When you genuinely understand your true motivation, then you don't think about the sacrifices, you think about the excitement and exhilaration of achieving your dream.

When I was a little child, I dreamed of one day becoming a paramedic. I've often thought about why I wanted to become a paramedic. Was it because of my father, who belonged to this noble profession? Was it because it just seemed like an excellent profession? Was it because I looked up to this profession and wanted to have that same trust and feeling of being needed by others?

Maybe it was a combination of all of these reasons.

Then I remembered a time when I was a teenager at high school and had a nasty accident that involved being in the wrong place at the wrong time. I was in the playground and someone threw a tennis ball to someone else across the grounds and I happened to get caught in the middle. The tennis ball hit me square in my left eye and immediately, I fell to my knees like a ton of bricks. The pain was excruciating. I couldn't open my eyes or see out of them. It scared the hell out of me. All these thoughts were running around in my head, "what if I'm no longer able to see? What if I go blind? How long will I be like this"?

The teachers called an ambulance and when the ambulance officers arrived, I felt calm and reassured by their presence. Their actions were soothing and reassuring. They relieved my pain and told me, "you will be okay."

Wow, the feeling of overwhelming relief came over me.

Looking back, the dream of becoming a paramedic was rooted in the aim of making a difference in people's lives. The subconscious dream I had set for myself was enough to push me through the years. I suppose you could say it was the quintessential example of "never giving up."

I've set goals before, but this was like a subconscious goal I had set myself without even consciously knowing it. I could write a whole book on this topic, conscious vs subconscious mind, and how it can work for us or against us, but that's for another time.

My first attempt to become a paramedic was directly after finishing school at 16 years of age. I applied, but I received the devastating news. I was two centimeters too short. Can you believe it? So close, but so far. "Now, what do I do?" I thought to myself. I was lost. Being a paramedic was all I wanted to do.

**The universal law of relativity states;
"every obstacle is an opportunity to change
perspective and your life."**

Once I picked myself back up and pulled myself together, I applied for other jobs while working out what's the next step that will get me closer to my dream. I thought, "Okay, it wasn't meant to be just yet, but one day...one day, it will happen. Patience, Lyn."

I proceeded to live life, got married, have children and get on that 'treadmill of life.' I would often think about my dream, but doubt and fear would creep in. I'm too old now to apply (I was in my 30s). How could I do such a demanding job with four small children? My husband would never let me take time away from the family to pursue my dream. I'm not smart enough to even pass the grueling exams. "What if I get posted far away from my family?"

It was interesting how so many fears and doubts crept into my mind. Do you ever get negative thoughts when pursuing your dreams?

One day I was sitting in my office unhappy and disillusioned with my career and my life. I needed a challenge. I wanted to do something that would stretch me and make me a better ME.

Then a thought popped into my head "What if I re-applied to become a paramedic?" There was that dream again. I thought it had died years before.

It was only in my subconscious waiting for the right time to go; "heh, remember me?"

The thought scared the hell out of me, but intuitively I knew it was time. Time to give it another go. Regardless of the outcome, I had to give it another go. So, I called on my four-step process that I use to overcome challenges and hurdles (like I did when doing triathlons).

The passion to be a paramedic was bubbling up again like a volcano ready to erupt. I had butterflies in my stomach. My heartfelt like it was racing. Deep down, my soul was screaming, "yes, yes, yes." Have you ever felt like this when thinking about your dream?

My mind was racing.

"Okay," I thought. If this is meant to be, then things will flow. It will all happen with little resistance.

That doesn't mean to say I will have no obstacles at all. It means that whatever obstacles come along, I will find a solution quickly and easily.

And guess what?

It did flow.

So, I applied. And I was accepted.

Okay, the first step was easy. That's a good sign. The powers that be had deleted the height criteria (thank goodness I didn't have to resort to wearing high heel boots).

Then the next step. Physical test. Passed.

Aptitude test. Passed with flying colours. Does that mean I'm mentally okay? (Depends on the day!)

Panel suitability. Time to be interviewed by a recruitment panel. OMG, I was so nervous I felt like throwing up. I had to give myself a good talking mentally. I had to get my head in the right mindset for success (more of my mindset techniques later).

Woo hoo, I was accepted.

Okay, now sit and wait for the next intake. That could take up to 18 months.

Wow, okay, no stress. I can relax. Nothing will change for a while. The pressure is off.

OMG, two weeks later, I get the intake letter advising that I was to start with the next batch in one month.

F....k now, what do I do?

Now I have some big decisions to make.

The Sacrifices

I had thought about the sacrifices, but I didn't expect them to come so soon. Definitely "flow" in action.

I need to give notice to my employer.

I need to talk to my husband and kids.

Can they handle things while I'm away studying?

Reality hits.

It's interesting how I wanted this for so long and when it became a reality, it was so scary — I had so many doubts.

I tapped into my success mindset techniques to stem the negative thoughts that were rushing through my head.

What's your "why" Lyn? Why do you want this?

For goodness sake, Lyn, you have dreamed of this all your life. Stop being scared and jump in. After all, what have you got to lose? What's the worst-case scenario? What if you don't pass the exams? Or, if you pass and find out that it wasn't for you. You can go back to your old life where you're 'comfortable' but not 'thriving.' The life in which you were not living and challenging yourself, just existing and waiting for life to pass me by.

Oh yes, that was the pain I needed to leverage. Pain is a more significant motivator than pleasure. Let me give you an example:

I went through a tremendous amount of pain, grief, guilt, anger and shame in my childhood when my father committed suicide. I developed PTSD (post-traumatic stress disorder, although I didn't realize that I had it at the time). It wasn't until I was a paramedic that all of this resurfaced because I had subconsciously suppressed this painful part of my life. Being exposed to traumatic events opened that wound of my father's death all over again.

Now, I help people that have PTSD, depression, anxiety, addictions, mental illness, or who are just struggling with certain aspects of life.

Don't make this journey alone. Two heads are better than one. A wise man once said, **"To learn from your mistakes is wise. To learn from other people's mistakes is true wisdom."**

Okay, when you put it like that, Lyn, you have no option but to jump in "boots and all."

"Feel the fear and do it anyway."
Susan Jeffers (great book).

So I did.

The studies were intense.

Being on the road in an ambulance. Working in a town, I'd never even heard of where people sometimes didn't speak English. Having no idea what I was doing. Having terrible supervisors that thought their main objective was to give me grief. Making mistakes. Having doubts.

I felt like quitting so many times, having to pass more and more exams, missing my family, feeling homesick, feeling lonely, being exposed to threatening situations, seeing things that most people would never see in their lifetime, about how the other half lives.

But heh "WIT" (Whatever it takes), right? I may feel like giving up, but I'm not going to. I had to dig deep. I had to use all the inner tools that I had **(the four-step system MCBC mentioned later in the book).**

Eventually, years later, I became a fully qualified paramedic and was later training others to become paramedics. Scary thought heh?

I'm so proud of myself for sticking it out.

The feeling of achieving your dream is a natural high. Who needs drugs, right?

Attracting My Soul Mate

Have you ever wanted to be in a relationship where the person *gets you?* Where it just flows? Is it easy? They understand you "warts and all"? You can be yourself. Where you have similar values and interests, and being with them is such a joy?

Humans aren't meant to be alone. We're social animals. That's why God created Adam AND Eve. Now you may argue that it was to procreate and yes, technically, you are right. But it was also for the keeping of company.

Now some women may argue that it was because God realized the mistakes he made when making Adam and so he created Eve after learning from his mistakes (only joking).

If you are single and loving it, then that's great too. I loved my life when I was single. The question I will ask you is, "do you want to be single for the rest of your life?"

Many people I coach often say, "I would rather be single than be in a bad/wrong relationship." And I agree. I've had my fair share of wrong relationships too.

Do you know what's interesting about that? I don't see that as negative. It's a positive thing. Think about it!

If you hadn't been in those bad relationships, you wouldn't have learned what you DON'T want in a relationship.

Those relationships are there to teach us lessons about ourselves, highlighting that we have self-sabotaging habits that we keep repeating in each relationship.

The Universal Law of Polarity states that "everything has a positive and negative part to it. Everything has an opposite so that we can change negative thoughts into positive."

Let me give you an example:

When I was single, I noticed I was attracting partners that I knew weren't right for me. They weren't the type of partners I wanted to spend the rest of my life with.

I realized I was always compromising myself and what I wanted.

I would lower my standards, thinking, "I don't deserve any better" and "I'm asking too much" or "I have too high standards."

I'm an occasional drinker, and I don't smoke, but I would attract men that drank a lot of alcohol and smoked cigarettes.

I would make excuses that "it was okay" and "I'll change them," and of course, it never lasted very long. I put myself through unnecessary heartache and pain. The pain rocked my self-confidence even more.

It wasn't until I did enough inner work and healing with coaches that I realized, "Yes, I do deserve the best." I do deserve to have someone that meets my standards; it's okay to have high standards. It's okay to believe I'm worthy of someone who will treat me like a princess and special. Someone who will love and adore me for who I am."

That's when I asked myself, "what do I REALLY want in a partner?"

"How can I attract my ideal partner if I don't know what he looks like?"

"What are my standards?"

"What are my values that I won't compromise?"

"What are my beliefs, and are they working for me or against me?"

"What are my core needs that must be filled?"

In other words, 'what makes me tick?"

"How does that change when I'm in a relationship?"

"What are my self-sabotaging habits when I'm in a relationship?"

Let me give you an example.

When I was in a relationship, I would always put myself last. I was always trying to please my partner at the cost of losing myself in the process. I was a people pleaser. I would put his needs before mine. In the long run, this would eventually make me resentful of him and then hate myself even more. It was a vicious cycle.

So, my first step was to get a coach. How could I identify these destructive patterns without help? I needed someone that was on the outside looking in. Someone that was detached from the emotional baggage, so they could see clearly and help me see clearly.

These coaches taught me to make a list of everything I wanted in a partner. Every aspect - how this person thinks (their mindset), their emotional intelligence, physical characteristics, and spiritual beliefs. Most people make the mistake of only focusing on physical characteristics.

Then the next step was to change my thinking. I had to believe that I deserved such a person, honestly. To never give up on meeting this person, I had to do the inner work to BE this person before I could attract this person.

The Universal Law of Attraction states that "like attracts like."

This means that I was attracting partners to the level of my thinking, not where I wanted to be. If I just continued to grow me, then I would attract a partner that was at that level.

Law of Correspondence states, "what you think and feel internally in your subconscious mind, you create on the outside."

Let me give you an example.

Have you ever thought about buying a new car? You decided it was to be a particular make, model, and colour. Then all of a sudden, you noticed this car everywhere. You hadn't seen it before. It was always there, but you hadn't noticed it because you weren't focusing on it.

That's when I attracted my soul mate.

It seemed like out of nowhere, he came into my life, but it resulted from all the internal work (foundations) behind the scenes that made all this happen. You could say I was "setting the stage."

This person ticked off everything on my list except one. And believe me, this list was extensive — two pages long.

So, how's that for laser focus?

I knew from the moment I started talking to this person that he was the one. The exciting part was that I had travelled around the world on my coaching and speaking tour and I thought I might meet him on my travels, but in reality, he was back in my home town waiting for me. He had even lived in the same street as me at one stage and we knew each other from years before.

Conclusion

The lesson here is "**have the foundations in place.**" Once the foundations are in place, the rest becomes easy.

It's like building a house; you need to have plans in place knowing your design, your budget, the type and quantity of materials required, your timeline, the problems that may arise in the process ... all even before you start building.

My 4 step foundations to pursuing and achieving your dreams are:

1. **M- Have a success mindset.**
2. **C- Know you're the 'why'- have clarity and understand the sacrifices needed to make it happen.**
3. **B- Understand your self-sabotaging habits/blocks.**
4. **C- Gain the confidence to implement changes.**

Believe in yourself.

Believe in the process.

Take action and be patient.

Achieving your dreams is the most rewarding thing you can ever do in life.

Yes, it may take some time, but it is **absolutely** worth it.

Just enjoy the journey along the way. **"It's about the journey, not the destination."** Ralph Waldo Emerson.

As long as you are taking little steps/baby steps towards your dream, it WILL happen.

Have faith, belief, trust and then let go.

The journey helps you become a better version of yourself. When you are a better version of yourself, you can be proud of yourself.

The law of cause and effect states, "everything happens for a reason."

You may not understand it at the time or notice it, but it could be years later that it all comes together.

Yes, you will go through many ups and downs; lots of doubts. Lots of fears will come up. All that is normal. If you don't experience any of that, then maybe your dream isn't big enough. It isn't enough to get you out of your comfort zone and stretch you. You will have roadblocks, but when the time is right, it should flow. Doors will open.

Many people don't know what they want and wonder why they never achieve anything. It's like a boat bobbing around on the ocean without a rudder. You're at the mercy of the wind, currents, waves, and will go around in circles.

I had a vision board and I would meditate on it and I would visualize what I wanted to materialize". It may sound a bit "hocus pocus" if you don't believe in this, but it does work. Many elite athletes today use this method to train their minds, which is just as important as training the physical body.

There is scientific evidence now that proves that the neuroplasticity of the brain is so powerful.

I do my "ME" morning routine every day. It's a series of seven exercises that have changed my life (I may write a book on this). Contact me if you want more information.

These exercises help me to de-stress, ground myself, stay calm, be at peace, focused, centered, and happy. A LONG way from my stressful days as a paramedic and running around like a "mouse on the wheel, and not getting anywhere."

Before learning and modeling what all the successful people do, I was a nightmare around, snapping at everyone; moody, and always stressed. I couldn't relax. I didn't listen to my inner knowing. I wasn't in flow (flow is where doors open and all problems and challenges are easily overcome).

I had to be in control of everything that drove everyone crazy.

Now I'm so at peace and chilled to the point I'm **more** productive.

Have you heard the saying by an unknown author, **"sometimes you have to slow down to speed up?"**

I listen to my intuition now and have a "knowing" deep in my soul.

I'm no one special. I'm just like you. I just decided I wanted to change things in my life and took **action** with the first step....**seeking help**, a mentor, a coach to help accelerate my success and learning. After all, why do things slow and hard if you can do it fast and easy?

Reach out to me. I would love to hear your stories about how reading this book has changed something in your life.

**"Keep your eyes on the stars,
and your feet on the ground."**

~Theodore Roosevelt

CHAPTER FIVE

Beyond My Wildest Dreams

By Beth Villegas

Dreams and goals can become magnets.
The stronger the goal
The higher the purpose
The more powerful the objectives are
The stronger this magnet that pulls you to that
direction – **Jim Rhon**

I was born in the Northern part of the Philippines, where the primary way of living is farming. I am the eldest of five children and a proud farmer's daughter of much loved, hard-working parents. Living off the land has a romantic feel, I love the connection to the earth; this life-style did come with a price and it broke my heart to see how hard my parents had to work. Farming in the Philippines is a precarious profession and all too often associated with poverty.

Often, the fragile beauty of clouds hanging low over rice-terraced hills is counter-balanced by the extreme weather that batters our islands with regularity. When a major typhoon occurs, it could easily wipe out a year's earnings! I witnessed the biggest typhoon growing up wiping out my parent's rice crops. It was so devastating that there was nothing to harvest for the next 12 months – nothing to repay the loans that they borrowed for the farm. But my parents are fighters and never gave up. They managed to get another loan and started all over again; never giving up, always with hope, gratitude and a smile on their faces. They planted corn, mungbeans and peanuts, in addition to the rice. Their hard work paid off, and mother nature was kind; brought relief and an outstanding harvest the following year.

Being a farmer is like being a priest; you take a vow of poverty and make a pact with the Lord that no typhoon will come and destroy your crops.

Plowing the land is such a strenuous and stressful work that no farmer wants his own children to become farmers. I witnessed my parent's hardship and suffering first-hand. Although they never complained and always showed grace and humility, I knew their dream was for their children to pursue more lucrative jobs, and not to face the daily challenges that came with living off the land.

My mother and father both came from a big family, with six siblings each. The best thing about having a big family is that you can always rely on them. We are a very close-knit family and we still support each other. Before my paternal grandfather passed away, he divided his estate equally amongst each child. My grandparents wanted to create a better future for all their offspring and prayed that their inheritance would help each of their children to be independent, and in turn, to give their children a better life.

Love and compassion overflowed in my home. My parents taught us the importance of values like kindness, resilience and gratitude; although they did not have a lot of material possessions, they were generous and giving, and always shared what little they had with others. They welcome strangers and vagabonds to our home. They hosted stranded families and business people by offering them a place to stay for free for as long as they needed.

A great gift from my dad was the appreciation and love I still have today for nature and 'the land.' Growing up, surrounded by rice fields, fruit trees, the beautiful smells of the fields, and fresh air. The memories ingrained deeply. I can close my eyes, recalling the feeling of grass between my toes, fresh air on my skin, rustling of the leaves on the trees, birds singing in the sky and the humming of the insects. I can even picture the beauty of the dragonflies vividly. I still remember the time that one of the dragonflies landed on my bedroom window. I slowly went near it and allowed it to land on the palm of my hand. I had a few moments of exquisite pleasure playing with this tiny insect before it flew off. I felt so much appreciation for God's creatures at that moment as I watched it fly away and find its destiny.

One of my fondest childhood memories was going swimming and diving with my cousins at the Cagayan River – the biggest river in the Philippines. We entertained ourselves by playing games, gathering shells and competing to find out who could collect the most beautiful shells. These are happy and treasured memories. Most of my cousins are now living in Honolulu and Maui, Hawaii. I have been blessed to have had the opportunity to visit a few times. My cousins not only opened their homes and their hearts, but also turned out to be the best tour guides. They were showing me all the beautiful tourist spots like the Diamond Head, Pearl Harbour, including a ride on the Atlantis Submarine at Waikiki Beach in Honolulu. When I was in Maui with the rest of my relatives, one morning, very early (3.30 am), we drove to see the famous sunrise in Halaekalae National Park. This mind-blowing feast of the senses was an experience I will never forget. We witnessed the magnificent first rays of sunshine rising on the horizon while standing above the clouds.

Another memorial adventure I experienced while in Hawaii was our trip to Hana in a four-wheel-drive vehicle meandering the winding roads and green landscapes. The drive to Hana was magical and amazing; driving along the coastline and green mountains on the winding roads gave us all a sense of total freedom. We stopped many times along the way to watch, admiring, enjoying and swimming in the beautiful waterfalls. Thinking back to these experiences makes me feel I was close to heaven, a feeling 1 will treasure for the rest of my life.

> **"There's a heaven on earth that so few ever find, though the map's in your soul and the road's in your mind."**
> ~Dan Fogelberg

As a teenager, I did not always appreciate the beauty of nature and the picturesque scenery that surrounded my home. However, they became my treasured memories when I emigrated to Australia. Memories of home would bring me moments of absolute joy, followed by the heartache of homesickness.

How my parents educated me and loved me were the two vital ingredients that created a solid foundation for my life to be happy and fulfilled. My parents were determined to give each of their children the best future that they could afford. They made sure that all of my siblings and I were educated to better ourselves so that we could create a future of prosperity, following our dreams and passions. None of us ever wanted to disappoint them and we all truly honored the sacrifices my parents made for us. We have all graduated from university and have all become successful in our own right.

**"Education is the most powerful weapon which
you can use to change the world."**
~ Nelson Mandela

I share my parent's passion for education. When I was
young, there were nights I could not sleep; I used to watch
the stars from my window and dream about the universe.
I would dream about my future. What job would I have?
Would I get married and have children? Where would I
live? On nights when it was dark outside and the moon
was bright, I looked for falling stars. Those were magical
nights filled with hope and longing.

Those nights of the falling stars were the most brilliant thing I had ever seen, it was like rain, but only imagined rain. Bright shiny blue sparkles fell from the sky, so
clear and beautiful. They say that every time you see a
shooting star, you should make a wish, which I always did.
My dream and biggest desire were to finish my college
degree, to get a job so I could help my parents financially,
meet and learn from other people, and spread my wings
to broaden my knowledge and widen my horizons.

From the very start of my education, I was determined to excel in everything I did. I put my heart and
soul into learning, and I loved every minute of it. I also
loved to be involved in various extracurricular school
activities and became class president, home economics
treasurer and secretary of the school body organization.
These responsibilities at an early age gave me confidence
as well as knowledge, and also assisted me in broadening
my horizons. I was chosen to be the leader of the school
delegation to represent our school and compete with other schools in the region. I wanted to be a role model for

my younger siblings, my classmates, my friends, and all the students at my school and neighboring schools.

Stepping out of my comfort zone made me even more determined and inspired me to follow my dreams and set goals for my future life – the very kind of life that my parents always wanted for me. I graduated with flying colors and had two gold medals as valedictorian of my secondary school. This resulted in a full scholarship grant to the university.

My prayers were answered; my dream had come true! Not only was I able to lessen the financial burden on my parents, but I was also able to fulfill their vision as well as mine. My parents were so proud. They firmly believed that we are affected by what we know and that we make better decisions if we are better educated. As the eldest child, I financially help my parents by supporting my younger siblings so they could study full time in college. As a result, all my siblings graduated from college. I firmly believe that hardship is not a hindrance to success; it is our stepping stone to success.

"There is no success without hardship."

~ Sophocles

My parent's struggles inspired me. They showed me that simplicity, family, grace and gratitude create happiness through dedication and humility; and that a can-do-attitude is vital for a life of fulfillment. A growth-mindset to always learn, wanting to know more, and always having a sense of curiosity and wonder, coupled with a positive mental attitude have helped me to become the person I am today. My parents wanted their children to have fulfillment without hardship, and the way to succeed was education. Farming is part of our history, a history my family is very proud of, but my dad especially wanted more for us, he wanted us to spread our wings, to discover the world and to bring change by becoming the best version of ourselves.

I did not want to disappoint my dad, dedicating my time to improving myself and helping my family. When I was 12, my family experienced a tragedy and my dad almost lost his life. The assault on my father had a profound effect on my life and changed me forever. I promised myself that, from now on, I would help my parents in whatever way I could. I was in year six and had started my first career, earning just five pesos per day (the equivalent of 15 cents in the US). I had to walk across several kilometers of paddocks and cross several streams by foot each day to reach my job site. Under the harsh weather – under the rain or glaring sun, my job in the rice field was to pull the rice seedlings with my bare hands and put them in bundles in preparation for the rice planting. Looking back, I feel that this was one of the most challenging times in my life. Still, it created a burning desire inside of me to succeed in fulfilling my dreams. It made me even more focused on my education, and soon afterward, I proudly graduated primary and then high-school with flying colors.

After my University graduation, I was feeling so blessed getting a job as a researcher in a small company. I traveled with my co-workers to different places, did inventories for various products and loved being in the field. This job gave me opportunities to meet different types of people who soon became my mentors and role-models, and showed me the opportunities and possibilities that I had never imagined.

I was head-hunted for my second job. An engineering firm, quite far away from where I lived, wanted me to work for them! I was intrigued and decided to go for an interview. The gentleman who interviewed me came across as very stern and severe, but he was impressed with my background. I was offered the position of Accounts Executive and to my delight, this job included a company car. My new job was exciting and challenging and involved extensive travel. I dealt mostly with directors of the company and heads of the safety departments. I can't begin to tell you how much I loved this job and how I appreciated the exposure it gave me to a wide variety of professional people.

Through my network, I was made aware of my next career opportunity, and I joined the military as a Civilian Employee at the Military Headquarters (GHQ), Quezon City in Metro Manila. As a researcher, I accompanied high ranking officers to visit various military camps. I also became the secretary of the Late Dr. Victor Valero, whose office was at the Malacanang Palace. I worked for the prestigious army organization that provides funding for military projects.

The Military General Headquarters (GHQ) was a vast military compound with very high concrete, barb-wired fences and eight scary-looking gates. Every single person entering the gate was checked before entering the site, and it almost felt like I was in a James-Bond movie, *from Manila with Love*. I loved my new "Miss-Moneypenny-role" and devoured the atmosphere, the manicured lawns, tall trees, greenery and the golf course. As a civilian employee, I was required to wear a uniform as well, but being a bit rebellious with my dedication to fashion, I used to wear my girly outfits as I loved dressing up. This would always get me into trouble. I received many warnings from my Commanding Officer, but I think he secretly liked the fact that I challenged the establishment and added some color to his day.

I also loved traveling with the high-ranking military officers, inspecting military camps and agricultural projects out of town. During one of our trips, we visited a pineapple farm and the sweet taste of fresh pineapple that one of the officers shared with me was heavenly.

Christmas time at Headquarters was always a significant event - all Military Families had the chance to relax, reconnect, and enjoy holiday traditions with their families. We enjoyed delicious, homemade meals, made gingerbread houses and had fun on the high and low ropes course. We went canoeing, fishing, enjoying evening activities, and of course, there was a visit from Santa and his elves – who must have been "alarmed" by our attempts to sing traditional Christmas carols.

Through my adventurous nature, I met very a kind, generous and compassionate friend who gave me ideas and encouraged me to travel to see the world. He showed me possibilities I had not even dared to dream. I began to see that there was a different life ahead of me, a life of much greener pastures. Through his help, I was able to fulfill part of my dream to see the world and I decided to call Australia my land of opportunity, my home. Australia is a fantastic place to live. It is the place that assisted me in realizing my full potential in reaching my goals in life and in making my dreams a reality.

To this day, I can still vividly remember the day I landed at Tullamarine Airport in Melbourne, Australia. It was 1 October 1986, the weather was perfect, the people looked friendly, and it was an ideal welcome to my new home. Although I pushed my initial feelings of home-sickness away, I was ready; ready for my next adventure, and ready for a new life.

Even though it was only a couple of hours stopover in Melbourne, these two hours had a significant impact on me. I felt positive energy, the excitement in me, and a new beginning was starting. I was ready to conquer and to face what lay ahead. My dream was coming true. I am proud to say that I now call Australia home.

My next stop was Sydney, a place I had only imag-ined from the movies. I recognized the beautiful build-ings, skyscrapers, famous landmarks like the Opera House, The Sydney Tower, the iconic Harbour Bridge and I remember feeling so lucky, blessed for the first time in my life – I felt like I was coming home, a dream come true. All my hard work, perseverance, focus and determination had made this a reality.

I arrived in Australia with just one suitcase; this suit-case contained all my worldly possessions. I knew very few people, but I loved the opportunity and challenge in-volved in making new friends. It did not take long before I had a new circle of people I loved to be with, beautiful, amazing and helpful people. One of these amazing peo-ple was a fellow Filipino lady who worked for Centrelink, a government agency that assists people in securing jobs. She introduced me to a small organization and got me a job interview. I was able to get a position as an of-fice administrator in a small company. A lovely young Canadian couple ran the company – the husband was the marketing manager and the wife was the promotions manager. The office was located in an amazing building right in the heart of Sydney. I felt so lucky that I had secured this job and somehow, I knew that I had entered the next stage of my life. I was excited and filled with gratitude and happiness – it was indeed a dream come true being in a beautiful, vibrant city I was surrounded by lovely, caring and easy-going people. I felt that there were tremendous opportunities and plenty of possibilities ahead of me. The universe was so kind to me, more than ever, I believed in the power of my prayers. As they say, "If you do your part, God will do the rest."

After work, especially during summer, I enjoyed taking the ferry from Circular Quay, and the fresh air and seagulls reminded me of home. Everything was going well in my life. The company I worked for expanded and moved to much larger premises out in the western suburbs at Parramatta, so I decided to move to a larger apartment close to the new office.

I was promoted, and I had a team working for me. Not too long after the company's expansion, the two managers I worked with decided to start their own marketing business and they asked me to join them setting up a news organization. I jumped at this opportunity and moved to a duplex house – across the beach from Manly – a short walk from Manly Wharf and close to my new office. It was a beautiful, vibrant location that suited my life-style. I enjoyed the challenge, but after few years, it was time to move on and I applied for a position at National Mutual Life Association as a Financial Officer in their Financial Services Department dealing with Superannuation.

Coming from Asia, I had never heard about Superannuation before, but I was ready to learn something new. The organization asked for someone hard-working and I knew I could fill that criterion, along with the combined skills I had obtained in my recent jobs. I was excited and curious to learn and broaden my knowledge and widen my horizons. I followed my intuition, secured an interview and was hired. I started with the company as a Financial Officer in April 1988. Working with this large, prestigious international company was way beyond my wildest dreams. I could not believe my luck and I loved my work. I was passionate about 'Super,' and I was like a sponge absorbing and learning all that I could get my hands on. I was promoted and my life just kept going from one high to another.

I also loved being a "city girl," as the buildings, the shops, the people and especially the view from my office was amazing. Taking the ferry home at the end of the day was like living in a fairy-tale, especially during summertime – life could not get any better.

That was until I met a Filipino, tall, dark, handsome, well educated, elegant and intelligent - my soul mate during a New Year's Eve party at my apartment. I call our meeting destiny as he was an "unexpected" guest who came along with a friend. We became inseparable after that night. We both loved sightseeing, eating out and driving around during weekends with friends. Six weeks after we met, we were officially dating, a couple of months later, he proposed over dinner in Double Bay, and we got engaged. He is a very private person, so a few only attended our wedding. My parents were unable to participate in our marriage as they still lived in the Philippines.

I was so happy and felt so blessed. Our marriage day was like a fairy-tale, a 'dream come true', and soon after, I was expecting our first baby – I knew then that God had been so good to me, I was so blessed and felt so very, very special.

The birth of my beautiful baby was complicated, but holding a healthy girl in my arms made it all worthwhile. I was a mother, another dream come true! Being a new mum was a whole new world, new responsibility, but I felt complete.

After six weeks of enjoying every minute of motherhood, I went back to work –my daughter went to a family daycare. Although I would have preferred to stay home longer, enjoying time with my little angel, I know, she was looked after and blessed having people around her who cared for and loved her as much as my husband and I did.

Juggling a full-time job and a newborn baby was a struggle, the mornings were especially challenging. I gained an appreciation for my mother over time and I also learned how to plan and to be super-organized. Although it was difficult leaving my beautiful baby girl in the care of others, I secretly also loved and enjoyed to be on the go and I was able to be highly productive.

A few years later, a day before my daughter's 2nd birthday, we went on a holiday to Perth, Western Australia. We were supposed to have a 6-week break but loved this tranquil city. It seemed like the perfect place to raise a family and so we decided to stay.

Another blessing and my prayers were answered again. On 15 April 1997, I gave birth to a healthy bouncing baby boy. He brought so much happiness, joy, lots of laughter to our lives and I felt my life was complete.

I was very fortunate and continued to work in the financial industry. I applied for a job as Risk Insurance Administrator for corporate clients, where I worked for more than 11 years. The company fully supported my education (Diploma in Financial Planning) and I loved my new-found hobby as a part-time student, with a full-time job and while being the mother of two small kids.

When it was my time to move on once again in my working career, I applied for a position at one of the biggest banks in Australia and was hired to assist two senior financial planners. One of the senior planners I worked with saw my passion, dedication, and work ethic, and when he was offered a position in a private bank, he asked me to join him.

A few years later, I received a call from a former colleague offering me a similar position for the biggest bank in the Southern Hemisphere; it was a great promotion and opportunity which I graciously accepted. I stayed with this prestigious institution until recently and enjoyed almost 12 years in the career of financial planning.

In February 2019, I received an invitation from the Philippine Department of Education to be the Guest of Honour and to deliver an inspirational speech to a graduating class, which I was delighted to accept. While I was in the Philippines, my first book, which was a book about happiness, and telling the stories of 12 amazing people, was launched. The book was another achievement and I felt very proud to share my journey in this world. Currently, I am working in a managerial position in the Finance Industry and I love my job. Considering my hard work, focus, mindset, passion, dedication and inspiration from my hard-working, as well as my loving parents, I feel proud of what I have achieved. I have achieved more than I ever imagined in my wildest dreams.

Looking back from where I came from, a humble family with plenty of love and support, I stepped out of my comfort zone to be a better person that is more compassionate, and I share my blessings to less fortunate than I am. I am a proud supporter of several organizations whose mission is to help less fortunate countries – providing better facilities for communities and schools.

One of these organizations is B1G1, also known as the Buy1Give1, a Social Enterprise that runs a global giving initiative helping businesses around the world embed giving in what they do.

Buy1Give1 has worked with more than 3000 businesses and changes the lives of millions. One of their initiatives included the planting of tens of thousands of trees. They also provide for millions of disadvantaged students to have access to education.

The B1G1 mission is creating a world full of giving, and now it's my turn to give back. You can understand why this is such a passion of mine. I can promptly assist others and share my good fortune by giving back and making a difference in the world, every day.

I was able to make the right choices and connections, as well as meet the right people to help me mold my future so that my dreams would become a reality.

As long as you have a dream, go for it with focus, passion, dedication and a mindset that nothing is impossible. Everything is achievable. Now, I can share my blessings, educate others and share my good fortune to the rest of the world.

"The secret to living is giving."
~Tony Robbins

"**To accomplish great things,
we must not only act,
but also dream;
not only plan,
but also believe.**"

~ Anatole France

CHAPTER SIX

From Waiting Tables to Becoming an International Keynote Speaker & Sales Coach

By Dario Cucci

As a child, I used to dream of becoming an actor, but then again, as I was growing up, I thought maybe I wanted to be a cook, or even a hairdresser; or perhaps a movie director.

But what I started realizing in my young adulthood was that dreams and goals could change almost daily, unless you have an intense desire to achieve them in connection to your Why. After the age of 26, I decided to move from Switzerland to Australia. My first goal was to learn the English Language, and then, after having stayed in Sydney for almost six months, I decided I wanted to live and work there to achieve my dream to become an actor.

Everything worked out fine, as I got a New Zealand citizenship because my mum is originally from New Zealand; with the agreement Australia has with New Zealand, I was able to stay and work in Australia. During the first six years, I followed my dream to become an actor, doing everything one can imagine to support myself while also studying the Meisner Technique at The Actor's Pulse for almost five years. Trying to become an actor is a tough job because it's underappreciated most of the time, and when you do finally get work, it's underpaid, too. Until you make it big on the movie screen or in a famous TV show, you have to work in other jobs to support yourself and pay for all the bills. So, first, I worked in the hospitality and retail industry, doing hourly paid jobs from topless bartender down to working at a small retail store selling supplements and doing additional admin work.

After the first year of doing odd jobs, I became a barista in Sydney through a friend of mine who was the manager. But the working conditions were not right, and after working with them for almost six months, an incident happened that changed everything for me.

You see, I am a very patient person and it takes a lot to get me to lose my cool. However, during that time, I was under a lot of stress. I didn't know how to control my emotions as I do now. I had completed many self-development studies and earned certification in NLP (Time Line Therapy) hypnosis, as well as acquired other ways of improving oneself. On that specific day, as I was working at the Barista coffee shop during my crazy busy shift, it happened that one table got free, and the next group came and sat down. I was running around cleaning up tables, taking orders and cleaning up again and again. As I'd just cleaned up one table for new customers to sit down, a couple of ladies in their mid-thirties sat down at a table that had just become free but was not yet cleaned.

This annoyed me in an instant because I had just cleaned a table right behind them, but they chose to sit at the messy one. Then, instead of being polite and waiting for me to find time to clean their table, the woman started to hassle me.

Knowing that I had my hands full carrying dirty dishes as I walked past them, one of the ladies called to me, "Excuse me, waiter, excuse me; can you please also clean our table?"

At that moment, I responded, "Can you please wait a moment? You see that I am the only one and I have my hands full. Her response to me: "You are so rude." I responded to her, "No, you are the one that is rude with your tone and calling me when you see that I have my hands full. I will be with you in a moment."

The woman didn't want to let it go and started complaining. "This is not acceptable; I want to speak with someone in charge."

At that moment, all I knew was that I saw RED. I went behind the bar where we put the dishes to wash and spoke to my supervisor; but instead of standing up for me, he agreed that the customer was right.

I'd had enough. I quit right then and there and walked away, feeling like a significant burden had been lifted. A sense of relief came over me as I'd never felt before.

I didn't have a job, I didn't know how I was going to support myself, but what I knew at that moment was that life isn't worth living if you work in a job that makes you unhappy just for the money. As I was very fit at the time and went to the gym regularly, I had this dream of becoming a personal trainer. So, after I quit my job, I remembered that dream and immediately enrolled in qualifying as a Level 4 Personal Trainer.

Over 20 years have passed since that time back in Australia, and I have achieved many of my goals along the way while creating new ones to make the ultimate life with the legacy I want to create.

Why am I starting with a story from my humble beginnings?

Because I want you to realize that you can achieve any goal you set for yourself. However, it might not come to manifestation precisely as expected. Since I stopped with the personal training business, I've attended many self-development trainings. I have received certification as an NLP Master Practitioner, Timeline Therapist, hypnotherapist, and DNA Advanced Theta Healing Therapist. I have also attended intensive workshops to learn how to sell from the stage, and I have become a professional public speaker.

I did all of these over the years while selling high-end programs within the self-development industry from such coaches and mentors like Tony Robbins, Chris Howard, Kerwin Rea, and Jamie McIntyre, to name a few.

After doing this for over ten years, having moved from Sydney to Melbourne where I worked with 21st Century Education for five years, I decided to start all over again by moving back to Switzerland. Back in Switzerland in 2011, I had to restart my career. I went from being a seasoned and well-respected salesperson and coach to starting over in a call centre agency. While working with them and after a short period of working with a startup company, I decided to start my own business.

Fast forward to 2019, and since then, I have started my own business, On-Call-Business GmbH, as a sales coach, sales trainer, and event's organizer. I have achieved a lot of my goals that I'd never thought possible, such as becoming an international speaker and bestselling author of *Crossroads to Clarity* and *A Journey of Riches: Making Changes,* and having published two books under my name: *Turn Your Customers into Profit* and *Crossroads to Clarity.*

I have a successful business that is growing, and my next dream is to have my upcoming event, The Ultimate Entrepreneur, to be a sold-out event that people talk about and recommend to their friends. I will hold this event soon, in 2020, in the USA and Canada after the London event that I am holding on the 2nd and 3rd of November 2019.

However, wanting something and getting it are two different things. I've realized over the years that things aren't always going to happen the way one has envisioned.

For example, I am running The Ultimate Entrepreneur Event now for the fourth time, and every time I hold it, it becomes better, but it's still challenging to get people to attend.

When I held an event in the past, I found that I could count on at least 30% of registrants to turn up, including even the ones that had FREE tickets. That isn't the case anymore. These days, even with all the marketing, phone calls, and texting, only 10% of FREE ticket holders show up to a self-development event. Low show up rates makes it very hard to fill a room, which is the main reason why I decided that for the fourth time when I am running this event, I will not be the only one responsible for filling the room. Also, people coming to the event will have to pay for the tickets.

Without the financial commitment attached, people don't value the content they receive from experts who have years of experience to share. The materials must be taken seriously so that participants can move forward in business and life, and create the destiny they always wanted.

And when it comes to having the right kind of people to be crew members, believe me, if you don't have that, holding an event is a nightmare.

The first time I held The Ultimate Entrepreneur back in January 2017, I planned everything out in detail, even got printed shirts for the crew.

The venue was in London City at the Holiday Inn Forum, and all the printed items, such as forms, wristbands, and so on, should have been delivered one to two weeks before the event date. Because I wasn't staying at the hotel, but across the road, despite my clear instructions to the hotel staff to hold parcels delivered, and the fact that I paid a lot of money to hold the event there, the hotel staff refused to accept the packages due to policy. They sent the printed material back without informing me.

On the day that I held the event, the enrolment forms were missing as well as the wristbands. We had to improvise. So, the night before the event, I called one of the keynote speakers and told him my dilemma. He helped me to get invoice/receipt books and brought along stickers for the attendees to wear.

The next challenge was that the hotel didn't set up the room the night before as they had agreed to do three months beforehand, because they had another function booked in that would go until 1 a.m.

After the prior function finished, they then started setting the seminar room with the stage. As you can imagine, my anxiety levels were through the roof! I wanted to make sure everything would be ready when people came to the event.

During that time, I was very stressed, to say the least, as I stayed up until 4 a.m. to make sure the hotel staff would set up the room correctly with the chairs and the stage. Then, at 6 a.m., I woke up again after having slept two hours or so. I got ready and met the event crew.

I thought the nightmare was now over and things would stop going wrong.

"Boy, oh boy, was I wrong again!" Not only were certain crew members late, but out of the five crew members I had hired to help out, four of them felt they needed to act out and behave like five-year-old children.

We had a meeting. I trained the crew on what needed to be done, from indicating when the speakers' times were up to controlling who could go into the coffee/tea room that had been set up only for VIP guests, to how I liked the registration table to be managed and even who would need to be in the seminar room during the speaker's presentation to assist or to attend the sales table.

I trained them on everything diligently, not only on the day, but we had also had a meeting via Zoom about what the crew would need to do during the two-day event a full two weeks before the actual event.

All of that preparation only to have them turn up and act like spoilt children saying things like, "I am not talented enough to watch the timer on how long the speaker has left and then hold up the sign to let them know." or, "I don't want to be at the registration table; I'd rather be in the seminar room and watch the speaker." or, "I don't want to tell the people that don't have a VIP ticket not to go into the coffee/tea room."

And they would argue over every point. I am a very calm and patient person. I have experienced a lot in my life so far, so to get me angry takes a lot. However, on that day, when the crew acted out like that, I lost it not only once but three times during the weekend. Yet I found a way to use what happened somehow in my presentation with a sense of humor, sharing parts of it with the audience.

The second and third time I held the event, I had learned to qualify better the people that wanted to crew and, as a result, those problems wouldn't occur again. Furthermore, the printing dilemma didn't happen again either, and I ended up hiring an event manager so that I could relax a bit and focus on being a keynote speaker and host rather than having to do everything myself.

But even with everything working well, free ticket holders didn't show up, and some of the sponsors were angry with me. Even with my improved marketing, everything done by the book, the third time I held the event in Heathrow back in February 2019, it was the lowest turnout I had experienced.

I was devastated and thought to myself, "Why is it so difficult to get people to attend an event?"

But that weekend, I gained a lot of learning, because the true colors of each speaker and sponsor showed up. See, when you hold an event and things go well, everyone will love you for it. However, when things that you can't control don't go well—Fact is, we can't control public transportation or people turning up on time to an event—it is in that moment when you see the true colors of those who are part of your event and how they handle the stress of it.

Out of about 14 speakers, of which ten were the main speakers who also promoted their services and products from the stage, only a few of them showed up with empathy and offering to help to make the next one a success. This also made me realize that I need to qualify the people I want to surround myself with when I hold events. And one thing I want to be surrounded by is entrepreneurs and experts who know how to handle themselves when things don't go as expected—people who will be supportive and understanding towards the host of the event.

After the failure of my event, I took time out for myself and literally was in bed for one week feeling sorry for myself and recharging my energy. I knew this would pass but didn't know when. After one week, I started having conversations with the people that were involved in the Ultimate Entrepreneur of February 2019.

However, I still didn't feel like I wanted to continue coaching my clients or hold longer meetings; it took me almost two months to get back on my feet, as I'd had a mini burnout.

During those two months, I reflected on it, took time out to look after my health, and even started doing boxing and Brazilian Jiu-Jitsu to get out of my comfort zone. I wanted to start doing something healthy that also could give me the body confidence to defend myself if I ever needed to.

And I went to a nutrition consultant to get advice on how I could improve my diet and lifestyle so that I could reduce my body fat, which was over 27% at the time.

Plus, I had help from people in my network who reached out to me, as they had noticed that I wasn't doing well. They offered their support. Even with all my experience as an NLP coach, hypnotherapist, Theta healer, and all the other techniques I've learned over the years, I still needed outside support to get back on my feet.

When you are in the deep end with depression and exhaustion, you can't seem to think or even see straight. So, I am grateful to Ben Ivey, who offered to do a coaching call with me using NLP to get me one step out of the emotional down that I was experiencing.

That one coaching session helped me accelerate getting back on my feet, stopping the victim mentality and becoming my hero again, taking action in a major way.

After that coaching call, I started going to the gym again, held more conversations, started cooking for friends and family and looking at the positives of what I can learn from the challenging time I have gone through with my event. I also started holding coaching sessions with my clients again and enjoying life more.

As a result, doors started to open again. People reached out to me, and I began to plan for the fourth Ultimate Entrepreneur Event. But this time, I spent a lot of time reflecting, planning and changing things around with the way that I want the event to proceed.

This time, I qualified the speakers' involvement not only from a financial standpoint but also from a perspective of why they would want to be part of it, what they would bring to the event to make it a success, and how each speaker could be an investor with their time, using their strengths by helping during the preparation phase and selling tickets.

One thing that I realized is, sometimes to create goals and implement them, we have to allow ourselves to be patient. The universe doesn't just drop something into your lap simply because you have an idea of when you want it to manifest, but it will do so when you are ready for it.

This also means you need to align yourself with the right people and be okay when something turns out differently than expected. Focus on being in the flow and take significant action to make it happen.

And if that means you need to cancel an event date or change venue or even take a break from business until you are ready to hold the event again, then so be it.

My event, The Ultimate Entrepreneur, is about helping business owners who provide a service get unstuck from experiencing *Ground Dog Day*, where they can't seem to take their business and life to the next level no matter what they do.

So, my promise to those who attend the event is that I and the other six speakers and coaches will work with each attendee during the two days to get them unstuck and moving forward. This individual attention is to help each one to accelerate his own personal and business growth, to enable every entrepreneur to take it to the next level.

And I believe that with what I went through myself in creating and holding this event, I am the Ultimate Entrepreneur, and you can be, too.

To be an Ultimate Entrepreneur, one has to accept help from other coaches and experts who have experienced those growing pains and are willing to share it with others.

Remember, you never know what will be the trigger point that helps you get unstuck from where you are right now. Still, one thing I can promise you for sure is that you only get unstuck when you get out of your comfort zone, ask for help, surround yourself with people who can help you, and then take significant action in applying yourself differently.

I hope that by sharing my story, I will inspire you.

And to finish it off, I want to share with you some additional tips to create and achieve your goals.

The essential aspects of manifesting your goal are that you need to have a vision with a loud Why.

I always had this vision of me standing on stage inspiring, educating, and entertaining thousands of small business owners, helping them to become better versions of themselves so that they can serve their customers with more confidence and increase revenue for their businesses without having to spend lots of money on ad campaigns or chase down new customers, or having to sacrifice their health for it.

It's important to me to leave a legacy that will live on long after I am gone, a legacy to make the world a better place. And since I don't have a family in the ordinary sense, my work, the people I coach, and the impact I like to have with my work is in a philosophical sense my family that I create, nurture, and grow.

For me, failure is not an option; it's just a stumbling stone that is in my way; something I can remove and still succeed with my events and coaching business.

Because I know that and because my Why is that strong, even during the darkest of times when I am thinking of giving up, I won't give up; instead, I will get back up, learn from it, and apply myself better.

Here is a framework and strategy that worked for me when I had to overcome challenges:

1. **Take time out and do what's best for you: meditation, fitness, hanging out with friends.**
2. **Reflect and write out the learning from your failures and what you can do differently next time around to make it a success.**
3. **Start working with coaches and mentors who can help you along your journey, and those who understand what you are going through from their personal experience.**

4. **Don't just attend seminars and forget about them. Instead, attend workshops and apply what you have learned to your life and business.**

5. **When in doubt and during the time of being overwhelmed, ask yourself these questions to bring you back to the now: What do I need to stop doing to prevent myself from sabotaging my goals? What do I need to start doing more of to support manifesting my goals?**

Believe me, when you apply yourself using these five tips, things will become a lot easier to manifest. You will learn to start living in the moment while learning from the past so that you can create a better future for yourself and your loved ones.

I do hope this helps you along your life journey and that reading my story has inspired you to do better for yourself, and to believe in yourself.

"**Trust in dreams, for in them is hidden the gate to eternity.**"

~ Kahlil Gibran

CHAPTER SEVEN

My Life Viewed from The Perspective of My Soul

By Leon Beaton

My life for the past thirty-two years had been unique as a secondary school teacher. I loved teaching and had no intention to leave the profession. I had planned to teach until I was sixty-five, top-up my superannuation and retire gracefully. But my soul had other intentions, which was about to be revealed.

"You should write a book about what you teach," one student enthusiastically told me. I never saw myself as an author, having failed English in year twelve and receiving a damning Teacher's College report for my poor English expression and lesson plans. But the idea of writing a book had been planted. Twelve months later, my teacher's aide said, "What you teach, you need to share with the rest of the world." Was there a message my soul was trying to convey to me? Is it to leave teaching? Write a book? But my doubts beclouded any possibility of writing a book, and I didn't wish to leave teaching. After all, it gave me great joy and satisfaction, but my soul wasn't going to surrender easily; it was going to make sure I received the message and acted upon it.

The Mystery Woman

I had been studying Neuro-Linguistic Programming (NLP) and had made close connections with numerous people; one of such persons is named Jackie. We had arranged to meet, but she surprised me by asking if she could bring along a friend. "By all means!" I responded. Her friend, in her fifties, and dressed in a long faun coat, colorful scarf, and matching beanie, looked directly into my eyes and expressed with definiteness, "You are to write." What did she know that I didn't?

My Soul Whispers

I couldn't ignore the messengers anymore. With the decision made to write a book, "Go to the lake and start writing," whispered in my ear. Two hours later, I had the title, "Desire – Connecting to your Divine Inspiration," and an outline of the content for each chapter. It's strange how events of my life happen to enable me to discover aspects of myself I never knew were buried.

A Messenger From God

Six months later, I was on a celebrity cruise in the South Pacific with Dr. Wayne Dyer and Cheryl Richardson from Hay House. I had no idea who I would be sharing my cabin with, but I intuitively knew it would be the right person; and indeed, he was. His name was also Wayne, whom I later called, "The messenger from God," as he delivered many clear messages — one being, "Get that book out. They are waiting for you to finish it." My soul was making sure that not only do I write the book, but I also publish it.

My soul was about to play its trump card to ensure that I left teaching.

The Camp

Each year, I conducted a camp that was called 'High Challenge,' and, as the name suggested, it was challenging! I had often asked the manager of my department to come and witness the different aspects of the camp. This particular year, my manager came. What followed became a choice point for my life. The manager took over the running of the camp. To describe the experience as driving a V8 car in first gear would be an understatement. The philosophy of the camp was changed entirely. I was frustrated, angry, and disappointed for my students.

"You should write a book about what you teach." "What you teach, you need to share with the rest of the world." And now the frustration of the camp. Those were three clear messengers I could no longer ignore. My soul was taking me in a different direction, but I didn't know where. This was the beginning of a long road of trusting my intuition and surrendering to my soul's guidance. From my soul's perspective, I understood the character my manager played.

My Soul Answered

While still teaching, I contemplated the meaning of the three messengers. I went to the school principal to ask for six months off as a service leave. He asked if I would take twelve months. To my surprise, without having the time to reflect on an answer, my body blurted out, "Yes!" Where did that come from? Again, my soul was guiding me.

When The Teacher Is Ready, the Student Appears

The phone rang. A lady said, "It has been suggested that I contact you to coach my son, as you have a reputation for working with troubled youth." I met with him and yes, he was troubled, but he wasn't interested in seeing me. What matters is, he came into my life for a reason. On a soul level, we had a contract. I was his teacher, and he was my teacher also. I was challenged to utilize the techniques to reframe his perceived negative experiences of his life, as a gift. As I saw the positive changes in him, I understood the gift he was to me and still is till this day. My soul knew exactly what it was doing: I was now facing a turning point in my life.

The Door That Didn't Open

My mind had expressed clearly that I could conduct workshops and mentor new teachers. I had the ability, and was respected for my skills. There was a definite need to assist new teachers. Diligently, for four months, the 'Teaching Excellence' program was created. After testing two of the modules with new teachers and receiving very positive feedback, I was ready to market the program. Over several months, I visited most of the secondary schools in the diocese. The response was that they couldn't afford it. My ego inwardly replied, "You know this is needed, but training your new teachers with me isn't your highest priority." I wasn't prepared to give my intellectual property away; not after what I had invested in myself to gain the experience, knowledge, and wisdom.

Not deterred, I launched my 'Teaching Excellence' program. I invited all the principals, vice-principals plus the first, second, and third-year teachers in the area. At the launch, no teacher was present except the few from my school, for emotional support. But to my surprise, sixteen of my former students appeared. The message was clear. My soul was saying, "You can try all you like, but this door isn't going to open. Look who's here — young men and women who appreciate what you have to share." I was beginning to see the path of my life, heading in another direction. My soul was saying, "You can keep knocking on this door which will not open, or acknowledge the sign right before your eyes and allow that to take you on a new journey of self-discovery." I chose to take a new journey. My soul smiled.

Decision Time

Long service came and went. Do I return to the classroom, or do I continue down the road I had chosen to take? Indecision! Courage! Trust! I decided to ring my principal to register for Emergency Teaching. That would provide an income while I continued to pursue what direction my soul was guiding me in. But my soul had other ideas. It wouldn't allow me to pick up the phone. It didn't matter how hard I tried; I just couldn't. My decision was made; it was time to resign from teaching. My soul had its way.

Financial Cord Cut

What now? My soul had taken me well and truly out of my comfort zone. For 33 years, I had been a classroom teacher with a salary that was delivered once a fortnight. Not anymore. I went from $90,000 to $20,000. Life was about to take me on a journey of major highs and lows — ego versus heart intuition, fear versus trust. And this was only Day 1 of the decision. Where was my soul leading me?

Instead of waiting until the end of the year for my farewell presentation, I received it in February. I still remember the words of the teacher's farewell speech. "Leon is the one who has taken the road less traveled." Little did I know how far that road would take me and what I was about to experience, let alone continually discover who I truly *am*.

Another Messenger From God

On a second cruise in the South Pacific, while attending two programs: one with Dr. Bruce Lipton and Gregg Braden, and the other with Doreen Virtue, I met a lady who really intrigued me. There was something mysterious about this woman, but I couldn't quite put my finger on it. At the end of the cruise, as we docked in Sydney, I said to her, "There is something about you that you're not sharing; who are you?" She went on to explain her life's work. My curiosity was correct. Later that year, we met again. She shared one life-changing directive. "Create a student manual of all your work to conduct workshops for the young people you can help." On returning home, I immediately set about creating the workbook. A month later, it was done.

One Door Leads to Other, Leads to Another

"You can do the NEIS program for starting a new business," I was told. As I walked into the Centrelink to investigate the possibilities, I sat amongst people who were waiting for their appointment. The energy in the room was extremely low and draining. I felt for these people. Then the idea hit me. "These people should be doing my program!" At my meeting, I was assigned to an Employment Agency but couldn't complete the NEIS program due to my positive financial situation.

At my appointment with the Employment Agency, they felt very confident they could find me a job. But it wasn't a job I desired. I wanted to conduct my programs. The Agency recognized my skills and even suggested I could work there. My soul said, "No."

But a door did open. The CEO of the Employment Agency was once a football umpire who umpired games I played in some thirty-plus years ago. I had also taught his son, and he was the bank manager who lent my family the money to build our restaurant twenty years earlier. After explaining my program, I was given my first opportunity, but that was six months away. What was I to do in the meantime? My soul had another ace up its sleeve — a colleague of mine.

A Friend From My Early Days At Teachers College

I reconnected with my friend Mike, after approximately 25 years. He was now the CEO of an education and training organization for people with disabilities. I rang him. The tone of my voice was a mixture of desperation, conviction, and forthrightness. I screamed down the phone, "I just need someone to believe in me and what I have to offer!" This led to a meeting with one of his staff. Mike didn't tell his colleague of our association, and rightly so. I had to gain this work on my terms. The result was I conducted my first six-week program assisting a mixture of gender and age to be empowered to take control of their lives. The river of my life was beginning to flow. My ego was satisfied, but also getting carried away with envisioning a bigger picture that could potentially play out.

My Contact; The Umpire Had Left

Some doors open and close, while other doors were like going down a rabbit hole, only to come to a dead end. Such is the journey of life. My soul was testing my resolve. Intuitively, I knew I had been called to leave teaching for a higher purpose. My soul knew. I had to trust the process and learn to calm my ego and listen to my intuition. The challenge was explaining to my family and friends what I was doing. They knew me as one person; now, they are seeing me portraying another. The label didn't fit. My relationship was being affected, as I couldn't give a clear answer to what I was doing or where my life was leading me. But this was my journey. I had to walk it and see where it led me.

Back to the employment agency, there was a new manager, Jack. My soul knew precisely where this was leading me even if I didn't. I had taught Jack's son. I looked him straight in the eye and said, "He was a brilliant kid. It's just that most teachers didn't understand him." These words touched him deeply. Someone knew and understood his son. This program was predominantly directed to young, unemployed men. Little did I know the door of this experience would open.

Patience On A Large Scale

As a result of meeting Jack and conducting the program, he introduced a colleague of his who worked in a training organization. We designed four powerful six-week programs for unemployed youth. The programs had to be submitted for government funding; little did I know it would take two years to receive a positive answer.

Another Door Opened

A very talented man I'd met through my NLP studies introduced me to a colleague of his, resulting in the next six-week program predominantly directed to unemployed women of all ages. All three programs were successful as defined by gaining employment and/or going on to further studies.

This was the last of the six-week programs that I conducted. My ego found it hard to be dealt with, as I felt this was the area of work I was to be involved in. The programs were successful; why couldn't they continue? It was the system. The government would provide funding for a program and then it would stop. I had to wait until further financing was made available from different government departments to an unemployment agency or training organization to conduct an appropriate program. My soul saw this differently. Complete one task, then the next one would appear, but not to stay in the same field of work. These were all stepping-stones to some higher purpose.

A Man I Felt Compelled To Speak To

Sometimes in one's life, a person crosses your path that you know you need to connect with. Briefly, this man's ability to see other dimensions and know a person's DNA lineage challenged my perception of myself. He shifted a blockage in me that allowed me to move forward with more certainty and confidence. As I stood before him, he thrust his right hand into my chest as if to grab something in a very forthright manner and said, "Get that fear out of there," and vehemently threw it away. The feeling of lightness was instant. He added, "You need to go to Egypt to collect your codes." Codes? What did that mean? I didn't know.

When The Student Is Ready, The Teacher Appears

While conducting a program in a suburb of Melbourne, I had another phone call from my friend, Jackie. The pattern was about to repeat. She brought along a friend she wanted me to meet. This lady, Lyn, became my spiritual mentor for some years. The first thing she did was ask me to organize and conduct a weekend retreat. This retreat taught me to believe in myself, put my notes away, and trust that the appropriate words would flow at the right time. She held the space for me to discover who I was becoming. My ego was beginning to release and allow my intuition to take control. All the years of my training plus the best of my coaching experiences went into this retreat. These participants wanted to be there, which, as a result, bought a different energy. In the end, I had formed a new belief of who I was becoming and what spirit would deliver through me if I put my ego to one side.

A year later, Lyn said to me, "You are to go to Egypt to collect your codes." This was the second time I had been told to 'collect my codes.' After much discussion of who I had been in past incarnations in Egypt, I said to the Spirit; Spirit, "You had better clearly show me that I'm to go to Egypt." Within a couple of weeks, I received an email about an Egyptian pilgrimage with two places left. I sold the last of my shares, which paid for the trip. This pilgrimage was to open the next chapter of my life.

On returning from Egypt, my body went through significant change. Great pain filled my body to the point that it was challenging to get out of bed, let alone walk.

I forced myself to walk to hopefully ease the pain, with little effect. My body was going through change at the cellular level due to the Egyptian experience.

Questions filled my mind. My relationship had ended. Where was I to live? What was I to do now? I had always wanted to live in Daylesford, as I loved its energy. I found myself a house-sitting job in the bush, ten minutes from Daylesford. The place was perfect. My accommodations were settled, but what now?

A Past Teacher Delivers An Answer

"Leon, will you please produce a book with your photographs and reflective statements?" pleaded a fellow teacher who followed my work on Facebook. It was something I had always desired to do — message delivered. Three months later, three photography books with reflective statements were completed. "Life – Is a Mystery Unfolding I, II & III." This was the next stage of stepping up and sharing my work in the world. The vision I had for these books was to provide something positive and uplifting for people to view and reflect upon while in a doctor's waiting room or waiting for an appointment.

"Leon, You Really Have To Meet Dorotha!"

On returning from Egypt and sharing my adventure with a friend, she said with authority, "You really need to meet Dorotha!" Yes, indeed, I did. She trained me in Reiki, levels one and two; skills that I didn't understand until in Turkey where Spirit worked through me to heal a man in great pain. I was only beginning to understand and remember the healing gifts I was blessed with.

Lyn Appeared Again!

"You are to conduct psychic readings!" I had already dipped my toe in the water but hadn't embraced it wholeheartedly. Again, my ego filled my head with fear and doubt. But my soul knew the bigger picture. I started conducting readings in the country of Victoria with varying degrees of success. Success defined by how many readings I conducted. I observed what other people were doing and started to compare myself with them. My ego was doing a great job of planting doubt in my mind. After evaluating other readers' talents, I asked myself, "What do I have to offer?" Slowly I started to form a picture of who I thought I was and what I had to offer. I created a banner that read, "Psychic Readings with Compassion, Empathy & Integrity, Incorporating Life Coaching and Mentoring." I also added my qualifications and changed my approach to the readings. Instead of worrying about how many readings I conducted, I began to focus on what I had to offer and trusted in the notion that whoever I was to see would be drawn to me. This is exactly what began to happen. My soul knew what was occurring. The more readings I conducted, the more I learned about myself and what I had to give. Continuing to fine-tune how I did the readings — with compassion, empathy and integrity — became my primary focus. I wanted people to leave, feeling empowered and lighter, and to begin to take control of their life.

The Market That Opened
The Door I Never Expected

"Oh, my God! You're Leon Beaton; let me tell you the story."
The relationship I had for ten years had just ended and I
wasn't in the emotional space for a new relationship. I was
at the local Sunday market selling my books when this
lady walking past, stopped and exuberantly expressed the
above words. This was the beginning of a spiral dance of
powerful personal awakening, transcendence, and intense
gratitude. The relationship was mutually beneficial — spiritual growth and healing at a deep soul level. We were
married in a past life, which ended tragically when she,
pregnant with our second child, drowned under disastrous
circumstances. It was a relationship that I greatly treasure
for the personal growth and healing that occurred.

Time To Step Up

A thought has been planted in my mind: conduct readings at the Mind Body Spirit (MBS) Festivals in Melbourne
and Sydney. But who should I contact? I found myself conducting readings in a small country town and shared my
thoughts with one of the ladies who had previously conducted readings at MBS Festivals. One thing led to another,
and before long, I had the guy's mobile number. The lady
said, "You won't get in; he has all his readers." I thought to
myself, "If I'm meant to be there, I will be" and then let it go.
On Monday, I texted a long message outlining who I was
and what I did. Tuesday night, I received a call. For over an
hour, he questioned me all about my work. The following
night, he rang me and said I had two days of work at the

Melbourne MBS. I knew then that my soul was directing me; I was meant to be there. This began the next stage of my soul's evolution. Something I never saw coming when I left classroom teaching. It was becoming clearer. I was still a teacher; it's just that my audience had changed.

Events Happen In Three's

Three has been a significant number to me all my life. I was born in March. I frequently stayed in places for three years or multiples of three. I had taught for 33 years. Even the number plate on my car, 228, reduces to three. When three separate events happen in rapid succession, I know my soul is trying to gain my attention.

The lease on the house I was renting was up. My partner and I had separated, and suddenly the contract I had for my work had ended. There they were: three events in quick succession. After processing the pain of the contract ending, I looked for the higher meaning of the three events. My ancestral home, Scotland, was calling me. Within a month, I was there.

Being in the United Kingdom for six months, a large percentage of the time in Scotland activated and reminded me of my spiritual gifts; one in particular – healing. I was beginning to understand the higher reason as to why I was called to be in the UK. My son said to me, "Dad, you've spent all the money to be there, why don't you go to Europe?" Since an early age, I wanted to visit Lourdes in France, as well as Assisi, because of the prayer of St. Francis. In recent years, the Camino in Spain had captured my interest along with connecting with Mary Magdalene in the South of France. Added to that was my love of Rumi, and traveling to Turkey became a must. All of the above was experienced in nine months.

Certainty In My Life, Or So I Thought!

On returning from Europe, I reconnected with my previous partner, but after six months, the relationship ended for the last time. We both knew we couldn't fulfill our soul's purpose if we stayed together.

At the time of our relationship ending, I looked into finding a place to house sit while I regained my thoughts and how my life would proceed from that point. I posted a notice in the local Facebook grapevine, and within five minutes, I had a response. The place was 33 minutes away. The position was mine. Within half an hour, I had another call to house sit. This call was to have a more significant impact on my life than I first thought. After meeting the couple, I was introduced to the wife's sister. Following a brief conversation, I left. Three hours later, I received a call; the sister wanted to discuss a proposal. "Come to the Yarra Valley and house sit my place while I'm away working," she said. This was a perfect position, or so I thought.

Everything Was Lining Up

When I returned from Europe, I received a phone call from a man who wanted to discuss my plans for a Centre for Education and Healing. After an hour-long conversation, he looked at me and said, "Your vision is so much bigger than mine. I have 25 acres of land in the Yarra Valley that I bought to do much of what you are describing. We can collaborate to build the place." This seemed perfect.

But life has its way of doing things. The place I was asked to house sit was no more than ten minutes from the man's land. After many delays of over a six-month duration, I finally arrived to house-sit the Yarra Valley property. Everything was unfolding perfectly until the owner, due to no fault of her own, had to end the arrangement. But where to from here? My frustration lasted about two days. It had taken me six months to arrive here and now it's ended. Having house-sat before, 'Let's try again,' I thought.

An Answer Arrived

Within a week, I had two places in Beechworth over seven weeks, followed by a three - month sit in NSW. I was being challenged to go with the flow. My soul was taking me on a journey that required me to surrender again and trust.

Beechworth was to become a place of realization that I could never have imaged. My Dad's words, "It's bigger than you think," rang through my ears. What was about to unfold would bring clarity to me like never before. The events unfolded like this.

1. I conducted a coaching session with the man from the first house-sit. I was given a tortoise as a gift. A tortoise always carries its home with it everywhere it goes…interesting.

2. I walked into a coffee shop. A lady shared a few words with me regarding her life. I chose to ask a few inquiring questions, which led to meeting her partner and conducting relationship counseling. A fortnight

later, their relationship was back on track.

3. Chilton opened another door. I met a lady who only three weeks earlier, opened her shop. My soul nudged me to ask her, "How can I assist you in promoting your business?" This led to a question and answer evening, followed by psychic readings and a reiki session.

4. While in Beechworth, I received a phone call from my son who forcefully challenged me to buy a motorhome and travel to Australia while doing my work. The seed was planted.

5. A friend of mine who sells beautiful crystals rang me on her way to a psychic expo in an NSW country town. After a brief conversation with the organizer, I had a stand at the event. Two experiences revealed how my soul was showing me the healing gifts I had and how to utilize them. Firstly, a reiki session using crystals and then medium-ship.

6. A dear friend of mine supported my son's suggestion and said, "Instead of people coming to your 'Centre,' you should go to the people."

7. All these events forced me to stop and contemplate why I had such experiences. I reflected on a session I had with a Medium in late December, where my Dad came through to explain creating a network of Centres, not too dissimilar to the World Wide Web. Looking back now, I started to understand the essence of that guidance.

I was already creating a network. Over the past four years, I had traveled to many country towns and cities in Victoria, Tasmania, and NSW, plus the UK and Europe, doing what came naturally for me: life/spiritual coaching. I loved it. It flowed from my heart; it wasn't like doing a job, it was a joy. To see the change in people after they left me was all the reward I needed, and now it was smacking me squarely in the face to continue what I was already doing, only this time in a motorhome.

Time To Act – Message Delivered

The intention is one thing; the action is another. After inviting a supportive friend to hold the space for me, we went to Wodonga to investigate motor-homes. By the end of the day, I found the vehicle. The Universe will reveal how it's manifested. During the day, the signs from the Ascended Masters kept coming.

1. The number 33 appeared to me three times within an hour. I know the spiritual world speaks to me through numbers, so this was a visible sign of support. According to Joanna Sacred Scribe, "33 is a Master Number (Master Teacher); all things are possible, guidance is connected to the Ascended Masters; any positive change or projects you are considering will be worth your while and you will be assisted in the undertaking."

2. The number 333 then appeared to amplify the message.

3. A truck drove by with three interlocking ovals with the word 'Trinity' in it.

4. The model number of the motorhome was C7932SL. Each letter corresponds to the frequency of three, and the numbers add up to 21, which reduces to three.

5. Being a person who loves the Hero's Journey, I pulled a card to confirm the day. It was #22 "For this, you were born." The card also mentions "Dream Symbol: Baby" That night, I dreamt of having a naked baby handed to me.

The message was delivered. My soul is now challenging me to gather my energy, creativity, talent, and willpower and cross a new threshold of adventure.

"A year from now you
may wish you had
started today."

~ Karen Lamb

CHAPTER EIGHT

Dreams Within Dreams Within Dreams

By Lynette Gehrmann

Building a dream, for me, is a little like writing a book. To write a book, we aim for an essential experience for you, the reader, to take with you on your journey. And so it is for building a dream.

Let me be a little clearer. To know what I was creating for you, I began with a statement of intention: I aim for you, the reader, to be inspired while reading—inspired to take action, strong in the belief that, if it comes from the heart, then a path will open up before you. A path in perfect randomness, delivering the ideal opportunities, step by step by step, in unexpected ways.

My aim for you is to know the power imbued with trust, the power of higher intelligence in us all. This higher intelligence has a more magnificent view of all the components required to breathe a dream—or a book—into our physical reality. All you need is a desire and an ability to let go and trust. And planning then will come from an inspired state of being.

The desire happens of its own accord, the beginning of a dream becoming dreamed. Letting go is something we may have to learn to do, to develop and practice. And trust evolves as we learn through our journeys that remarkable things happen along the way—remarkable stuff we could not have planned for in our wildest dreams. Depending on the dream you are creating, planning will occur with a little focused intention and lots of inspiration, maybe right from the start or perhaps sometime later.

I want you to know that the journey is what creating a dream is about before a dream can take a stronghold and manifest. Enjoying the journey is paramount, as is for me enjoying the words as I write. Enjoying the ride brings together the cooperative components, the rendezvous with the perfect people—or the perfect words—to take you on to the next step.

It is the Universe scattering another component, and another, and another, individually or in clusters—or thoughts, ideas, and words—on your dream-inspired path. Doors of opportunities are opening in unexpected ways. This is the path of inspiration. When the perfect opportunities present themselves and action is taken, then trust and hope and positive expectation and passion become the fuel that drives you. A fire within is ignited.

And, so, this is the way I approach writing a book or a piece of work. The title is the dream. The intended experience for you, the reader, is a journey of learning and inspiration — the same as the path toward a vision. And the completed work is the creation of a dream. So, let us continue.

Who Am I?

Besides being an author, who am I and what do I know about building dreams? My name is Angel Knight. Well, that's not true. Angel Knight is my pen name. My real name is Lynette Gehrmann. It is sort of like living a double life. Living life as a play, you might say. To be able to play with the idea of a dream is an important skill to master. It takes an attitude of a childlike quality — an openness to newness, a curiosity to see what inspiration unfolds. And then it's time to put it away, pack it up in a box ready to pull out another time when the inspiration leads you to peek into the box again.

This is an excellent way to describe how I became an author. I had a dream at the age of about fifteen or sixteen to grow up and become an author. I don't know how the idea came about. It was merely an idea that sounded good. It hung around for a while but never really took off; and adulthood took over, and the thought of becoming an author lay to rest for the next thirty-five years. I never seriously thought I would ever write much of anything. But a dream is like a seed and sometimes, but not always, a seed lies dormant before it begins to sprout. For example, a bamboo seed will lay in the earth for six years before it shoots up, then overnight grows tall and strong. This is how I experienced becoming an author — like a seed that lay dormant.

Through life, we all have many dreams. Dreams within dreams within dreams. Each dream branches off in specific directions and will cleverly interlink with one another. I dreamed of becoming a mother and a wife. I did. I dreamed of traveling to exotic places. I have. I never dreamed of living a life filled with trauma and struggle, but I did. And oddly enough, it was the unwanted life lived, which led to a must-achieve dream for me to be healed of pain and suffering, which consequently led to realizing I had a story to write. And suddenly, the seed which had lain dormant for decades began to sprout until it became an absolute reality that, one day, I would write a book.

The knowing was strong, and it grew stronger until chance brought about all the cooperative components which supported the birthing of my first book, *Ascension Battlefield*. I hadn't planned the timing of it, and our dreams are best not to be rigidly planned. Planning and action are required, of course, but only at the perfect time with inspiration moving through us. Dreams can be restricted from the benefits of spontaneity if we put too much focus on planning and take action, which is not inspired action.

While some dreams are like a seed, a tiny desire which lies dormant until the right time, other dreams are born from a powerful desire to see change, because the status quo has somehow created a trauma. I know this because, besides writing a book to demonstrate I had walked through the fires of hell and had reached a consistent state of peace and having absolute knowing and clarity that if I can do it, so can you; with the trauma of myself and family, a powerful desire was birthed. Hmmm, that was a mouthful to say. It was a long, birthing process.

Through my own lived confusion, I was both consciously and unconsciously asking for clarity. In asking for clarity, and having the desire to feel no longer the emotional pain I was experiencing, I had created a desire to understand. In the desire to understand, I was led on a path of personal healing. Personal healing with a desire to understand led me toward becoming a healer, guide, mentor, and spiritual teacher.

I had a conscious awareness of what it means to be a spiritual being having a physical experience. This was the second part of a dream I had, which was birthed from one very profound spiritual experience in particular. It wasn't my only one. I had searched the globe for answers and, in the process, discovered I also now could help individuals with mental and/or emotional trauma. From all of this, another dream has been dreamed.

So, you see, a dream can be like a forgotten seed which suddenly emerges, and then you know that one day it will bear fruit. Or an idea can be something that happens to be an underlying driver for your whole life. Identifying what type of dream you have will determine how you handle the emotions and thoughts around it when emotional and mental challenges come up.

Depending on the depth and breadth of your dream and the importance you place on it, your capability to handle the challenges will vary. The part all dream creation has in common is learning to let go of the dream of becoming physically actualised. Actualised in a see-it-hear-it-touch-it, tangible kind of way. You see, once a dream has been created, it already is real. It already exists. Granted, not in a 3D sort of way, but a goal is already real as an idea, and the way to see it manifest is to let it go.

And this is where trust comes in. It's not easy to let go of a dream that is very important to us if we believe it doesn't yet exist. However, if you can consciously understand that a dream has to first exist in a holding place or a dream state before it can become a physical reality, then you can manipulate your subconscious into being happy about having it. The subconscious then sees it as already real.

To the subconscious, everything is real, but if we believe a dream has not already been created, then sometimes it can be tough. Tough when we want it so badly. Think of an idea as if it is a pregnancy. You know you're going to have a baby, but you don't *have* it yet. Not in a way that you can hold it in your arms, but you trust that a baby is coming. So, a dream is in a state of pregnancy. And it can come to fruition.

What Is My Biggest Dream?

As I briefly mentioned, I have experienced struggle and trauma. When mental health is not understood as spiritual, and then a spiritually gifted, creative, and intelligent growing child one day begins to struggle with suicidal thoughts and confusing visions, the love a mother has for her child will drive her to find answers.

However, as it came to pass, I had to heal my internal pain and suffering first. In the process of healing and gaining clarity, I discovered I have my gifts, which I never understood, and I awakened gifts I never realised were possible. This brought me to understand my spiritual self more deeply. Sometimes we are so much more than we know we are.

So, somehow, over time, through my life journey, a dream has grown: a dream to see mental and/or emotional health understood as spiritual. Extrasensory perception is something we can all develop, and intuitive medicine is the way forward. Bit by bit, I am making a difference. I am teaching individuals to understand their inherent natures. I am helping people to heal themselves of their traumas. I am clearing confusion and demonstrating that, no matter what a person has been through, he can completely transform his life like I have. This has been very rewarding in multiple ways.

One day this way of thinking, of understanding mental and/or emotional traumas as having a spiritual component will infiltrate our health systems in a big way. This is a dream I know I will be working on for the rest of my life. And even though it is exciting, still, as long as mental and emotional health is not seen from a spiritual perspective, individuals will fall victim to a system that he doesn't understand. This causes its own kind of trauma.

There is a long road ahead. To be at peace with what is, inspired to go forward and able to let go while also trusting takes patience and knowing my dream is possible. With this attitude, I am meeting people with similar dreams and different skills. The attitude of knowing a dream is possible is a compelling point of view to hold. The ripple effect is strong and will grow stronger. If you are reading this and you know someone who has a similar desire for change in the way mental and emotional crisis is viewed and treated, then please send them my way. From here, anything is possible.

From my life experiences, I have a knowing—a knowing which only grows stronger; a knowing that there is higher intelligence, a greater intelligence which knows how to help us bring our dreams to life. So, trust for me became easier and more comfortable over time. Call that intelligence God, if you will, or call it the Universe. Call it All That Is. Call it collective consciousness. Call it Source. Call it the power of creation, Law of Attraction.... Call it whatever feels best to you. If you have this kind of belief within you, then you will understand what I am talking about here.

Ask for what you think you have to have. Ask for what you need. Ask for clarity. Ask for ideas. Ask when it feels right to ask, and then let go. As I have found myself unexpectedly asking here for example, asking my readers to send anyone passionate about change in the way mental and emotional crises are viewed and treated, I have done so from an unplanned part of this writing. It came from inspiration.

This is how we walk the path of creating a dream: moving forward with spontaneous, unplanned and inspired action now and then. It is allowing the magic of life to move you in unexpected ways. Sometimes there are immediately obvious results, and at other times, it takes time. Time weaves its magic. Learning to trust that time will yield its magic may not happen right away. Of course. So, learn to flow a little; don't hold on too tight, and see what time-space brings to you.

Allowing the Dream to Grow and Blossom

Who each of us is today is a culmination of all we have lived through. I once wrote: We are the total collection of the life experience we have had. We never are away from the pain of our past. It may go to sleep for a time. However, it is always there and can sometimes show itself quite unexpectedly. It requires acknowledging, recoding and/or healing, to then enter our life book of wisdom. Never ignore anything. It is all a part of what you take forward with you.

It is from the wisdom that we step each step toward creating our dreams for real. Wisdom is born from experiences of our past. Much knowledge is derived from resolved pain. Although we haven't *only* experienced pain in our past, if we don't transform it, then our suffering will act towards sabotaging our dreams. Intelligent action is subtly influenced. Addressing the painful issues which occur again and again in our lives is vital. They come into our lives now, shown to us in unexpected ways, because of our past.

Putting peaceful closure on that which has ended can be done in many ways and becomes a part of something you have learned to let go. This, too, adds to your life experience. As you go forward, those times when youagain need to let go of a painful feeling will be aided by the very fact that you have successfully let go of something before having another life experience to draw from positively.

The steps toward creating our dreams are, however, not only about wisdom and knowing how to let go. It is even more critical to have experienced life joyfully. A past filled with joy and passion and things which felt right to you is the ingredients the Universe uses to put together synchronistic events of absolute delight. Every good-feeling moment counts, and what an enjoyable experience it is to be delighted with synchronistic events.

Perhaps you haven't had much joy in your past, and if so, NOW is the time to start. The joy factor of our entire makeup is an essential factor of actualising our dreams in a wanted way. It can seem like we are wasting time if it has no direct logical connection to what we want to create. However, an unmanifested, fully actualised dream lives in a holding space, and who we are moment to moment, becomes a component of that holding space. For example, it took me personally experiencing struggle and trauma to activate and bring my first book into being. It was a book which had to be written. *It* led me.

My dream as a fifteen-to-sixteen-year-old was actualised. Had I chosen a more exciting path with more adventure and good feelings, that too may very well have led me to write. After all, it feels so natural to me now. My first book would have, for sure, been a whole different story, though!

When we can get past the apparent logical route to specific outcomes—but not ignoring the logical completely—and allow our imagination, our inspiration, plus our pure joy of life to be a part of our guiding light, then we allow the unforeseen to bring us magic. The collective of components and how they will be put together are massive on the subtle level. We cannot predict everything from our narrow point of view. We aren't consciously aware of everyone's life experiences, dreams, and desires, which will put a particular person or persons on our path.

We can't see around corners, either, because we are living in an experience of linear time-space dynamics. There is a greater collectivity of human experiences, dreams, and desires which come together through the laws of creation — multi-faceted. There are laws of physics behind it too grand yet, for our scientists to understand completely. So, this is where learning to trust in our inklings and intuitive knowledge no matter how slight, will over time, show us its Truth colour with some logical common sense of knowledge, which is something we also need.

The major key to remember is, if it lights you up, then plan, plan, and plan. If not, then know within yourself something yet unseen has to come into play. It may be a particular person you are destined to meet, or it may be a specific experience that will spark an idea. It may be any number of things that need to happen before more detailed planning is called for at this point. Feeling within you a lightness, a joy, and inspiration which moves you, is the surest sign you are on the right track to actualising, which is more perfect for all involved, whatever dream or dreams you have.

In Short

Learn to let go; there are many ways to do this. If you are reading this, you are sure to know some.

If you feel what you know is not working, then ask—even if you must speak the words out into the air with no person listening. And then take a deep breath and do something else.

Enjoy life just a little bit more, and new energy will be breathed into greater potential for your journey of building a dream, being more personally rewarding for you.

Identify unresolved pain getting in the way as it shows up. Don't go looking for it, but do take note when it shows up. Then, at the soonest time possible, find a way to bring healing and resolution.

If it inspires you to write down your dream or dreams, then do so. Writing makes it more robust. Add, subtract, or alter what you have written if you wish to do so. Over life, we expand, become more complex and more precise about who we are and how we wish to experience our lives. With new clarity, we may benefit from expanding on what we have written before.

Take logical steps of action if it feels right and light to do so. If it feels heavy, yet you feel you still must take action, then make sure it is your best choice. In every action, there are always at least two choices. A reality of duality makes it so. Before taking action, in this case, identify at least two possible options and always, always, always take the lighter action. Trust this feeling of lightness. Lightness in body and heart. Therein lies higher wisdom.

And, finally, I ask you to reread the words I have written, again, at another time. There is energy in these words, which are coming from a higher wisdom, a higher intelligence that my conscious understanding cannot even fully see. When I read over what I have written, even I see something not seen before. I am often surprised. This is a gift I have received unexpectedly from learning to trust and follow the lighter feeling action — the most luminous feeling in body and heart. You will be surprised in many delightful ways too, along the way. And that is part of the rewarding and lovely journey of building dreams.

"The secret of change is to focus all of your energy, not on fighting the old, but on building the new."

~ Socrates

CHAPTER NINE

The Art of Dreaming

By Cindy Vazquez

I am a firm believer that life is about dreaming and about fulfilling our dreams. I was always a free spirit that is creative; and the type of child considered a dreamer. I remember being six years old, and I would stare at my hands, asking myself such questions as: *Why can I feel myself and touch my hands while it seems I am the only person experiencing this feeling?* I looked ahead of me at everyone passing by and wondered, "Do they feel as I feel when I look at my hands? Do they feel as if they are the only ones experiencing their lives? Am I just an observer of them being in my space? I am touching my hands and I feel my body, so why can't I feel their feelings or their experiences as I do mine?" There I was with enormous curiosity and wonder. My curiosities, awoken the desire and passion for exploring the world and traveling to many places.

I have had opportunities to travel to several places within the United States, Mexico, and Puerto Rico. Living in Puerto Rico has been one of many dreams I have been building on, and I am looking forward to adding more travel destinations. My husband and son have been part of this journey with me. Building this dream has been exciting, and my husband has provided the vehicle and opportunity for me to be able to do so. I am grateful and blessed.

As my husband serves our amazing country and, having been born in Puerto Rico, his career has provided me with the opportunity to explore and live on this beautiful island. He was assigned to serve in Puerto Rico from 2012 to 2015, and we are presently stationed in Puerto Rico once again to serve from 2018 to 2021. The news of our return to the island came as a shock to me, though. I loved visiting for vacations, but living here is a different perspective for me, having been born in the U.S. and being of Mexican descent. We speak various dialects of Spanish, for one thing. News of the impending move to Puerto Rico was nerve-racking for me. Puerto Rico was too far away from my home. For me, home is in the state of Texas.

The journey began for us in the year 2012, and while living in Puerto Rico, I was very resistant and negative. All I wanted was to go back to mainland U.S. I couldn't be open to a different culture than mine, and therefore, life in Puerto Rico became very challenging.

Ironically, I am one who loves to travel and experience other cultures, but here I was resisting. I did not appreciate the moment and the fact that life is not just about comfort, but also to observe, listen, learn and enjoy every moment and experience.

Fast forward to this present moment, 2019, I now know why the Universe/God (what I believe to be my spiritual guide) got me to go back once again. I genuinely appreciate those gifts; the gifts of listening, learning, understanding, but the most crucial lesson of all was to practice the art of less judgment—or no judgment—and to be fully present and see the beauty of Puerto Rico and its beautiful people!

I now enjoy the island from a different perspective. When I don't agree with something or even dislike it, I now practice compassion to the best of my ability. I practice patience. I feel I am more present and more at the moment.

These experiences have also allowed me to be a better mother to my son, showing him the beauty in the lessons when we are exposed to other cultures.

Living in Puerto Rico has brought me plenty of lessons, lessons I feel I am to learn and apply. As a child, my dream was to travel and see the beauty of the places I dreamed of visiting, but it never occurred to me that I would encounter a culture shock or resist the fact that people could be way different from what I have been exposed to my whole life. I believed that just because people in Puerto Rico spoke Spanish, they were exactly like me and would, therefore, understand my point of view or how I perceived life.

I also came to realize that just because I'd lived in the United States and was raised there doesn't make it okay for me to judge and criticize Mexico by comparing my current experience and place of residence to my previous homes and countries. I would question: *Why can't you understand my way of speaking Spanish? Why is it so hard?* This was when I discovered there are many different dialects in one language. Even English has many different dialects. Still, since I'm so used to Mexican Spanish and English spoken in the United States, I was, in all honesty, very ignorant, closing myself off from the opportunity to learn from an exciting experience.

I now understand the importance of being open and being flexible when it comes to different cultures and dialects, especially in the same language. One huge lesson I have now learned is to allow less judgment and be present with an open mind to understand and learn from anywhere. I get the opportunity to travel.

The journey we experience when we allow ourselves to dream is priceless, especially when that dream becomes a goal fulfilled in our lives. I have always been attracted to art, color, creativity and design. Art is in my heart, especially when it comes to color. I remember when I was in 3rd grade and our teacher gave us an art assignment to complete; a watercolor painting of whatever we felt inspired to paint. I remember grabbing the piece of white paper and watercolor paint, having no idea what I was going to create or paint but knowing that it was going to be very fun and relaxing. I painted trees and a background of great depth; the trees continued to expand into the extent of the paper, creating a 3D effect. The leaves were painted cartoon-style, but they seemed to have movement as if the winds were gently touching them, like a small breeze. The light green to dark green on the leaves made you feel as if the trees were alive every time you stared at the painting.

Once I'd finished the watercolor painting, I looked at it and said, "Wow! I added too much water and the paint might run all over the paper... or maybe not." I left it to dry for the next school day.

The next day, my teacher had all the paintings she thought were unique and creative on the wall for display. She congratulated all of us and especially those students who happened to have their creations chosen.

To my surprise, my watercolor painting, which I thought was not perfect or excellent, had a ribbon pinned next to it. I was awarded first place in my category of watercolor paint creation! My teacher came to me and asked me to stand in front of the classroom so I could be acknowledged and congratulated by all my classmates. I was shy and in disbelief. How was it possible for anyone to like my creation and award me first place? I was excited and happy for sure, but I couldn't believe it.

That moment was truly priceless and memorable. This was the moment I discovered that I was born to be an artist. The following year, in 4th grade, I created another unique work of art. This time around, I created a simple two-dimensional, almost three-dimensional artwork on paper. The creation was a big house like a mansion. I decided to paint, cut and glue each detail of the home, including furniture, construction paper and chalk. I remember it was time-consuming, but it was fun, and I knew it was going to be unique. I never knew my work was going to be chosen for an award again — art for me was a time to relax and have fun. I happened to arrive in class once again and found my creation showcased outside the classroom. I was awarded first place! I was honored and pleased; my self-doubt this time had diminished.

Since I had discovered art to be my talent, I continued to create small artwork for myself in art class. When I was getting ready to move forward into middle school, it meant a new chapter in my life and a brand-new middle school to inaugurate with my classmates. This was exciting, mainly because I was about to be part of my middle school's history as one of the first students to walk into that new middle school building! I knew right away that my extra-curricular activities in my new school were, for sure, going to include art class. I will never forget my 6th grade art teacher, Mrs. Cuyoo. She had a gentle personality and a love for art. I could immediately feel her passion for art and teaching. She made me feel welcomed. We were all excited about our next in-class project.

I remember once, after the school day, I was in her classroom while waiting for my mother to pick me up. I loved being in her class and learning more about her passion for art. She shared with me that her specialty was in drawing and painting. She could even draw a portrait of me right there and then if I wanted. I looked at her in surprise, disbelieving a teacher would take the time to sit down and draw me.

She said, "Sit down, Cindy. This isn't going to take long. You have such beautiful eyes, and the way you look is beautiful as well." I sat down in intense silence, still surprised. I didn't know if I was to smile or not smile. I can even close my eyes right now, seeing myself back on that stool in front of her desk, looking straight at her looking at me while she continued to draw.

She smiled when she finished and said, "Cindy, you are a gorgeous young girl. You came out just beautiful. Here you go; a gift from me to you."

I looked at the finished portrait, and I didn't think the drawing looked like me. This beautiful artwork was just too cute to be me. I smiled and said to her, "Mrs. Cuyoo, this is me? This is how you see me? Wow! I am too pretty here, but thank you." Later in life, I realized how insecure I was as a 12-year-old. I was indeed a beautiful young child.

Later that year, Mrs. Cuyoo gave us a project to complete in class. The project consisted of painting a Santa Fe home from an Indian tribe named Tewa. The house was to be drawn as they used to construct them before the Tewa were placed on reservations. She gave us the instructions and explained how the drawing was to be finished as a layered style painting.

I thought the concept was challenging, but I was sure it was possible. We started the drawing on white paper, then we were to place a transparent sheet of paper, especially for painting, on top of the picture. On the first layer, we were to paint the house. On the second transparent layer, we were to paint the background, such as the sky and far background details away from home. As I was creating my work, I was starting to enjoy it and to see its unfolding beauty and concept as unique.

I came to the last layer, which was to add the details of the sky, and I started with my already perfect mix of color to begin painting the sky. I completely forgot that I only had about forty-five minutes every time I attended an art class. I started painting the sky with beautiful light peach color, as I was looking to create a sunset view, but I had to stop since the class was over. The next day when I came back for class, I was looking to match the same color I had made the day before, but I wasn't successful. I kept mixing and mixing different shades of the color I had used the day before, but each stroke I added to the painting would not match the color. I decided to continue with the unmatched color because time was running out and I had to finish.

Several weeks passed and more projects were created and finished. Mrs. Cuyoo came over to my desk during one of those days in class. She gave me a huge proud smile and gave me a special invitation to an art award ceremony being held at the high school on Friday evening. I remember looking at her all confused and curious to know why she only gave me that special invitation. It turns out I was awarded 1st place in my category and grade in the school district. Wow! I was so thrilled that I was silently bubbling with excitement.

When I came to share the news with my parents, they were very proud and happy, but mostly, they were excited. They said they were not surprised because I was very talented and loved art.

The time came to receive my award, but before we attended the ceremony, we had the opportunity to see all the displayed artwork of the winning students. My mom and my aunt were the ones who had come with me. When they saw my painting, they couldn't believe their eyes. They had thought my work would be a straightforward drawing or a painting that a 12-year-old could only create. But it turned out that my painting looked as if a professional artist had painted it.

I looked at them like, *Why are you all surprised and shocked with disbelief at my work?* For me, that was a standard painting I was looking at; the same I used to paint during class. All I could see was the mistake I had made with the sky. I couldn't get rid of the fact that I knew I had made a mistake and it was not perfect.

When I shared my mistake with my aunt and my mother, they looked at me like, *Are you serious?* What they saw was a sky becoming cloudy as if the weather were changing. That part of the painting was unique; it was the highlight. I looked at them, surprised. I hadn't even thought about it, nor had I seen it that way. When I looked back at the painting, I saw what they were seeing, a sky having a change in the weather. It was interesting that it had turned out that way.

The time came for me to receive my award, first-place medal, and it was a proud moment for my mother and aunt as well. They were delighted, especially when they saw it was not just a child's painting but an actual artistic rendering. But mostly, they were proud because they saw that I had talent. This day changed my life in a big way. The experience of painting this piece taught me to trust myself and my heart a bit more. I learned I could create and accomplish anything I desire if I focus and create from my heart.

Mrs. Cuyoo was the vehicle for me to find one of my dreams; from that day, I discovered how much I love to create through art. I started to enjoy color and began designing new artwork. I then realized that one of my passions is developing art and using color. I knew that becoming an architect was one way to fulfill my creative dream, but I also loved color and texture.

In high school, during my 11th-grade year, I took advantage of the opportunity to take drafting design classes. I went into the classroom thinking I was going to start designing houses as soon as the teacher introduced the details of the class. I soon discovered we first had to learn the basics, which meant industrial design. This style of designing was boring to me, but it was super important to understand before even attempting to design a house or a building. I only took one year of drafting design when I decided not to come back for the second year.

Drafting design showed me the side of designing that lacked color. Since I knew I loved to color and texture with designing, I decided to go with interior design as my career and profession. Interior design had both the design and the color, plus textures and more. I remember, when in middle school, sitting in my art classroom daydreaming of one day becoming the most successful interior designer in the world. I grew up and life continued. I kept my love for art and design. I graduated from high school and went on to pursue my dream of becoming the best interior designer I could be.

My journey in higher education started in a community college. I started the plan, the dream, but then I became distracted with new experiences, new freedom, and meeting new people. I got distracted by going out, socializing and having fun with friends, and I had to find a job to sustain myself. This changed my whole point of focus and I forgot about my dream of becoming the best interior designer in the world.

Then nine years passed and I got married. My son came into my life and blessed us with his presence. This was when I decided to go back and finish what I had started nine years earlier. I went back to school to complete my associate degree in interior design. I graduated in 2011, and that was one fantastic feeling of accomplishment. I learned that if you don't quit on yourself and your dreams, no matter the journey or circumstances, those dreams are always possible. Taking action is a step, but persistence and faith are the keys to fulfilling all desired dreams.

Accomplishing my dream of earning my associate degree in interior design was a joyful milestone in my life. I am now transitioning back to my 12-year-old self. I used to love playing paper games with my childhood friends. One of the paper games we loved to play was called fortune teller. This game was a four triangular-designed 3D-constructed game. Within the triangular empty spaces, you were to write at what age you were going to get married, what kind of house you would have, how many children, what type of car, what city you were going to live in and so on. The purpose of the game was to predict your future, whether you were going to be married or be single and be successful in your career or business. It was a fun game, and we loved playing it most of the time. It was, in a way, exciting; it was a way to imagine and dream about our future as adults.

Of course, it was just a children's game; I never gave it much importance. I do remember, though, that every time we played the game, I would always answer I would be married by age 24. I was going to have only one child, and it was going to be a boy. I wanted a boy because I hardly had any patience for myself as a girl, having to be all nicely dressed as a girl was expected. I did not agree with most of what my culture and society were telling me to be, while boys could have it so simple and easy. It was all about playing fun games and sports, and that's what I loved to do. I loved playing with the boys in various sports, fun activities, and outside games. Whenever I was nicely dressed with my hair done, I couldn't play freely, and there was just too much time spent on getting all nice and ready. This was one reason why I always wanted a boy if I ever had children, and I only wanted one healthy boy.

I also used to say I would have a big home before having children. I used to describe my home as a two-storey house with three to four bedrooms, and it was to have a huge kitchen. Mind you, I did not like to cook, though, and I still don't want to cook. These were just some of the answers I would say when we played the game. The predictions usually were as I imagined or dreamed of them becoming. I always thought it was exciting.

As an adult, my priority at age 19 or 20 was not to get married or have children. My priorities were to be successful in my career, become financially independent, and be the best in my field. To a certain point, I did pursue the career part, but then I met my husband. At that time, I had no idea he was going to become my husband and the father of my only child. I believe we were meant to know each other and be in each other's lives. After dating for three years, we decided to get married.

To my surprise, one day, as I was preparing all the details of the wedding, I realized it was going to be my 24th year! I stopped and said, "Wait a minute! That was just a children's game. I am going to be 24 when we marry?" Yes, I was in shock. I had manifested the age I would get married. Yes, it was a children's game, but in a way, I had this unconscious dream and desire to be married at 24 since I was a child. I didn't have a particular reason why it had to be at 24; I just knew and felt it was going to be around that time. I was excited and happy; it was an internally joyful moment of realization. We got married three days after my birthday. We had a fantastic wedding accompanied by dear family and friends.

Two years passed, and we were on our way to purchasing our first home. The house was beautiful. It was a big house, a two-storey house with four bedrooms, two and a half bathrooms, a family room, dining room, living room, a den, plus a breakfast area and a big kitchen. The house was perfect; the irony was that it was only my husband and me. I have always had a desire and attraction to big spacious homes. A small house for me was like feeling trapped with no freedom. To this day, I am still attracted to significant spacious dwellings for the same reason we chose our first home. Even having the opportunity to purchase this house was a dream come true from childhood. I have always dreamed of living in a big house, and I came to realize this was another dream I had manifested from that silly game I used to play as a 12-year-old girl.

One year later, I was surprised by the news of my pregnancy. We soon learned that it was a boy! The news was so exciting and joyful to us because we both wanted a boy. I remembered my baby boy was bouncing all over inside of me. I still laugh when I go back to that precious memory. Once again, another dream manifested and fulfilled. I came to learn that nothing in life is a coincidence. You build dreams with your imagination and subconscious mind; you also have to believe your dreams are going to come true and they will!

Life is about building our dreams, no matter what part of the journey we are in. When I was a child and teenager, I would always say to everyone that I would be rich and financially free. I would move out of my parent's home at age 15 and have my apartment and be very successful in business. I always witnessed my family laughing or judging me like I was just a silly girl. Except for my mother—she has always believed in me and would say I am a diamond so polished that I brighten the sky. Mom would tell me not to let anyone diminish that brightness and to keep going for what I felt was right for me. Therefore, I am still building my dreams, and my dream of becoming a successful businesswoman is in the works right now.

Embracing the journey while fulfilling this dream as an adult has brought many challenges, but I keep moving forward in life. This time around, I have learned that failing is part of the journey; it is okay to fail if you are learning how to become better from those experiences. We are taught in school not to cheat and never to fail. I agree with working as a team in collaboration with others. I also believe failing is okay, but never to quit on your dreams.

When you improve and continue to pursue your dreams and goals, you are, in fact, a positive example to those who feel success isn't possible for them. This is where I stand now, to continue the journey of becoming a successful businesswoman, one that not only brings value but also brings the opportunity to be an instrument to better the community, city, state, country, and all of humanity.

I have realized that living in Puerto Rico has been a blessing in disguise and an awesome adventure and opportunity to explore its culture and its beautiful art, especially its unique Spanish façade architectural design. Building my dreams consciously, and even unconsciously, has been a fantastic path towards understanding myself. This path has been an exciting one with lots of joy and fun, but it has also been a huge roller coaster ride of emotions and doubts. I am often surprised when I go back to my childhood and remember how I dreamed of many amazing things that have manifested in my life.

Having a mentor, a teacher who loved her work, and the love for art allowed me to learn and dream that, one day, I would fulfill my dream and complete a degree in interior design. I am grateful for her and her presence at that time in my life. I am a true believer now that life is to be experienced. The ups and downs of the journey are part of life. They are the ones that make the dream more fulfilling and worth continuing, no matter what. I love reading this quote to myself when in doubt, and so I leave you with this.

"Promise yourself to be so strong that nothing can disturb your peace of mind. Look at the sunny side of everything and make your optimism come true. Think only of the best, work only for the best, and welcome the best. Forget the mistakes of the past and press on to the achievements of the future. Give so much time to the improvement of yourself that you have no time to criticize others. Live in the faith that the whole world is on your side so long as you are true to the best that is in you!"

~ Christian D. Larson

"**The distance between your dreams and reality is called action.**"

~ Ben Francia

CHAPTER TEN

The Nine-Step Dream-Builder Blueprint

By Narelle Burgess

"To live is the rarest thing in the world. Most people exist, that is all."
~ Oscar Wilde

Have you ever wondered why some people win in life while others continue to search for the instruction manual?

Through a lifetime of ups and downs, the successes and trials in my life, and an education obtained from the school of life's hard knocks, I believe I have discovered an extremely valuable blueprint for dream building, and I want to share it with you. The essence of this plan has been extracted and distilled from my own life experiences. I trust it will help others appreciate the opportunity to avoid painful experiences by following the wisdom contained within this simple blueprint.

I have created a repeatable system of processes anyone can follow. Knowing and understanding the Nine-Step Dream-Builder Blueprint can draw clarity and success magnetically into every aspect of your life, whether in your personal life, in business, in property dealings, or with investment decisions.

You could achieve your heart's desires, even your wildest dreams. You could choose the right goals instinctively. You could develop your failsafe GPS to guide you through life.

The System looks like this.

1. **Values**
2. **Reason**
3. **Create/Originate**
4. **Mentors, Mastermind Groups**
5. **Perspective**
6. **The Process**
7. **Gratitude**
8. **Letting go**
9. **Revision: Reflect, Refine**

But what does all of this mean? And does the order matter? Let's break down the steps in the order listed. Obviously, some of the steps will intersect, but the order I offer has significance. The first step, Values, is the most important step of all. This is the keystone that locks and binds the other eight steps together. Even so, all nine are essential to complete the blueprint in the most powerfully effective way.

Values stand as your compass or rudder—or, perhaps, even a map—without which, the result would be confusion. Without your rudder, you will turn in circles arriving at destinations that will not serve your greater plan. Whenever we are disoriented, when we wander off track, we are never at ease, always feeling that something is missing, continually searching for that which we believe is lost. You may ask how is dream-building useful to real life? How does it serve us? What are the benefits it enables?

My mum told me that I couldn't do certain things because I was not smart enough or rich enough. Pursuing excellence was not encouraged in my home. I've since realized that I alone must take responsibility for my achievements and abilities. I must become myown coach and reward myself on the road to achieving success.

Questioning myself while working through these steps helps me to know myself more fully. The more effort devoted to this task, the deeper the understanding and the higher the congruence. Synchronicity and miracles then begin to appear more regularly in life. This creates the freedom to be who I want—who I am—to become the best me for myself and my family.

Stuart Scott wrote, **"Don't downgrade your dream just to fit your reality. Upgrade your conviction to match your destiny."**

Are you ready?

Step 1: Values

Our values create the very keystone of all of our dreams. Values are the beliefs and ideals at the core of our being. When satisfied, our actions are congruent with our hearts' desires; we can then find happiness and contentment.

I've found that becoming clear on the things that are important to me is very liberating. Making time to know myself honestly creates perspective, linking every thought and action to my values, igniting goals, creating the most profound meaning from otherwise mundane, repetitious, or bland everyday tasks. This process leads to truly *experiencing* happiness and fulfillment. Values determine the purpose. Values come first. Then goals followed by action determine outcomes.

Picture a mind map. Core values are like the strong tree trunk supporting majestic branches (goals). Identifying my potential shows me opportunities and internal aptitude to fulfill my values. This is where it all starts. Now picture your mind map.

Research proves that reactive depression comes when needs are not met. The only way to fully understand our own needs is to make an effort to know who we are and identify what is congruent with our ideals and beliefs. Deep inside, we yearn for authenticity.

How do you determine your values? Think about your childhood pleasures. Take 15 minutes to remember a time when you believed you could be whatever you wanted, when neither time nor money was given a fleeting thought. This is where life started for you.

Begin by listing your childhood pleasures. This list might include spending time in the garden, playing with stones, or toy cars...any activity you enjoyed so much that you lost the concept of time, returning again and again.

Think about how these childhood pleasures are relevant to you as an adult. Do you still love spending time in the garden? Do stones still capture your imagination? Are you fascinated by motor vehicles? Retrace your childhood steps in a quest to find answers about who you are today. What do you still enjoy? Who do you want to be?

How quickly childhood dreams are put away in the eager rush and responsibility of being all grown up! I learned this the hard way in October 2009. If you had been with me then, you would have seen me burn out.

Practitioners believe I suffered a mini-stroke when I relentlessly pushed myself harder and longer during the Global Financial Crisis. We believe that we overcome challenges by working harder. We are *all* wrong!

Losing my cognitive functions and direction, I was then faced with the quest of getting to know myself all over again, to examine how I think, indeed even to be *able* to think and to weigh up what opportunities and choices were still available for me to work in some financially productive way at age 57. I found myself seeking fulfillment in a role where I could manage to thrive while having limited functionality because of health constraints. I was on a quest to find an occupation where I could be self-employed in spite of the inability to work for very long periods. I had limited resources and had lost my standing in my community.

I learned that acceptance equals change. Forcing things creates resistance. I had to figure out exactly what my values were so that I could develop laser focus, clarity, and direction.

This is why Step 1 is at the very heart of the dream-building blueprint.

Core values are the foundation of dreams.

Step 2: Reason

The second building block locks into the first. Without step 2, we have no strength or determination. However, with this step, our dream takes on meaning, and gains incredible strength. Step 2 is our reason born out of our values: our Why. It is the purpose that drives us. Our reason provides knowledge mixed with the power of emotion, creates our vision, our purpose, and then our goals become non-negotiable.

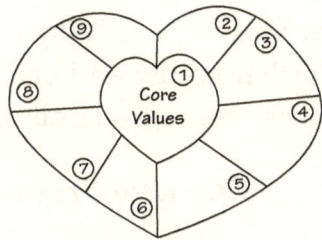

Why is reason so important? Our reason is our compass, our navigation tool, the great clarifier, the great sifter of wheat from unwanted chaff. Reason magnetizes miracles and synchronicity into our daily grind. Our reason is the fuel that helps us reach our destination. How can we reach our destination if we lack fuel, i.e., enough emotion and passion for lighting our fire? Passionate people produce!

What is my reason Why? Wanting to live in a home near the beach excites me, as does being a positive example for my family and my community. I want to enjoy financial freedom to fulfill my potential and the measure for which I was created. I want to be philanthropic, contributing to causes such as Microloans, Fred Hollows Foundation, Swags-for-the-homeless and of great importance to me, I want to develop affordable housing solutions for the young and mature aged. I am creating legacies and understanding for my family.

To achieve Step 2, we must find, clarify, and refine our reasons, becoming more precise and more concise daily. Every project or activity has a mini reason congruently reflecting our overall reason in life. Every day, every task, I ask, "Why am I doing this?" thereby gaining further clarity and ensuring tasks are aligned with purpose, vision, and beliefs.

Step 3: Create/Originate

"Everything is created twice, first in mind and then in reality." (Stephen Covey, from *The 7 Habits of Highly Effective People*)

How then, do we create? The creation begins in mind, with thought.

While meditating and pondering, I came to realize that each of us has opportunities to tend our thought gardens, creating and nourishing the most magnificent crops. I'm convinced, no matter where we start, we're able to reach the most fabulous goal or destination. We picture it into becoming real; as long as we are emotionally congruent, the mind builds the shortest bridge to make it true.

We must picture, meditate, and imagine. Thus, I am encouraged to proceed with confidence.

Drawing Sept 2017 by my inner child. An intuitive drawing of my peaceful place. Memories of childhood holidays with the family at the beach, my favorite place to be. Mum is under the umbrella; Dad is fishing in the boat. I am swimming with my younger sister and brother. The sun and infinity signs are significant.

"Whatever the mind of man can conceive and believe, it can achieve."
~ Napoleon Hill

I have found that knowing myself brings true happiness. Constant, diligent searching brings clarity, congruency, and great satisfaction. When we are creating, we are rewarding our emotional and temporal needs. Knowing how we tick and what lights our fire, we are better able to communicate our needs and likes with others.

The daily practice of meditating or praying for 15 to 30 minutes helps to enable this understanding. I've found that the first five seconds upon waking is most vital, as it influences the next five minutes, and so on throughout the day. The second most important is five to ten minutes before sleep. These are the greatest times for positive and creative thinking, meditating, creating.

Vital to the creation process is MINDSET-STRATE-GY-ACTION-RESULT. The practice of listing and regularly reviewing my vision and goals in the front of my diary has proven powerful and effective when combined with taking action. Listing important desires keep my vision and goals front-of-mind always. Constant daily focus creates an internal mental radar and magnetic force-field, attracting opportunities, and this is the most incredible navigator for life.

You have to start. You cannot wait for perfection. Refinement happens in the process of taking action and doing.

When I set and live my intention daily, I find power. By prioritizing my purpose, passions, and values—often pondering what I'd do if this were my last day—deciding how to live it—I find no time for procrastination. Today's the day. Now's the time!

"To live is to choose. But to choose well, you must know who you are and what you stand for, where you want to go and why you want to get there."
~Kofi Annan

Step 4: Mentors and Mastermind Groups

Without Step 4, we lack support, belief is limited, and we feel alone like the odd one out, a swan amongst the ducks. But with Step 4, we realise we're amongst champions, swimming in the right pond or flying in the right flock.

Why is Step 4 so important? Well, first of all, we like to fit in, to belong. However, we're most fulfilled when we're in the *right* tribe, spending time with people who are champions in their areas of interest. We're the average of the five people we spend the most time with at any given moment. So think about this. Who do you spend your time with?

Mastermind groups provide us with likeminded people, people we want to emulate, the people we identify with, our intellectual soul mates for want of better terminology.

When seeking to achieve anything significant, I've always had at least one mentor with wisdom to draw from. When flat broke, I needed them even more. I would purchase second-hand books or read about them on the internet, attend free or low-cost webinars, catch the train to free or low-cost seminars...whatever it took to gain from their knowledge and leadership.

I choose mentors whom I admire, people who can teach me more about whatever subject I am trying to master or advance in. I might choose Brandon Bayes or Dr. Eric Pearl when I'm studying health issues, or perhaps Mary Morrissey or John Assaraf, when trying to improve my mindset. Property mentors included Mark Ralton, Dominique Grubisa, Kevin Doodney, and Ian Ugarte.

Think about who you would choose to learn from, whose perspective you most admire for a given topic, and buy their books or research their teachings on the internet.

Mentors do not have to be currently living. Many great minds have left their legacies in print to be accessed long after they've left this world. My advice is to follow those who speak to your heart. But if you are starting out and can afford only one book, pick up *Think and Grow Rich* by Napoleon Hill. Reading this book regularly and applying its principles has created more millionaires than any other book. Apply it to any goal.

Step 5: Perspective

We can choose the meanings we attribute to events. Many inspiring people have turned their lemons into lemonade. The way I see it, if they can transform difficult circumstances into positive experiences, so can I!

My dear mum, a resilient woman who passed on in 2010, always said, "When you reach the end of your rope, tie a knot and hang on!"

While mining through my diaries recently, I found "A Love Letter to Myself," an exercise in perspective which I wrote in 2017 while trying to shine a positive light on my life. I find myself returning to this list of self-affirmations which have become very uplifting during challenging times in my life.

We're all able to choose our focus and the meanings we draw from events.

From my letter, I quote:
I start by saying thank you for your love of learning, teaching, and sharing, for being a mum who always strives to develop the talents of her children.

Thank you for being creative and artistic. You are very cautious and thrifty, making a lot out of limited resources when faced with financial challenges.

You're so loved from both sides of the veil.

I love you for seizing miracles and blessings without hesitation, with sure knowledge and determination.

Wrap up words of encouragement: Keep having faith in yourself and always remember, you're enough. You're a child of God with a grand eternal heritage.

Your family and circle of influence depend on your strength of character.

I love you, Narelle (condensed version)

My letter has many personal references to serious obstacles I've overcome. It reminds me that I can see the failures or I can see the lessons and learnings. My tenacity in overcoming very painful moments in my life has led me to a perspective of success and love and gratitude to and for myself.

By thoroughly enjoying the journey of life, it is no longer work. It stops being about how many times you fall; it becomes about how many times you get up and the lessons and strength you gain with each event. You could have little financially and yet be only one deal away from retirement! How you view life determines how or even *if* you see opportunities at all.

"The difficulty lies not so much in developing new ideas as in escaping from old ones."
~ John Maynard Keynes

Step 6: The Process

Step 6 is about the process. When we have Steps 1 through 5 in place, it is now time to build the dream through a bit of introspection. We must ask ourselves a few questions.

What materials do I have readily available for my Dream-building? *What do others say I'm good at?* To answer these questions, consider which of your skills and talents garner the most compliments or make you feel most fulfilled. My answers might range from networking and planning to writing, teaching, and coaching, to name a few.

What are the skills available for my new Dream-building? *What comes naturally to me?* Some of these answers will parallel with the previous ones. Here, I might answer networking, negotiating, organization, management, speaking, decorating, interior design and so on.

What does my Dream-building look like? *What would I love to see myself doing?* This is where we project the outcome we would like to see. For instance, I would like to travel around Australia and overseas, retracing my ancestors' origins. I would also like the financial and time freedom to do more with my family. I love to exercise regularly and take long walks, also to pursue artistic interests. I want to speak globally, to purchase properties and to have a couple of homes in different climates.

What life experience do I bring to the project? This is where you will consider your life experiences, particularly the problematic parts, and recognize the skills you've developed because of having gone through them. In my case, I raised five children, won awards for financial planning, and have worked in property development. From this, I learned to be an excellent salesperson, a good communicator, and have learned what it takes to create significant profits due to helping many people achieve what they wanted.

What are my potential Dream-building projects?
By listing my own experiences, skills, and interests, I see the potential to find gratifying work as a coach, a property developer, a speaker, or a facilitator of business/wealth mastermind groups. Think about what your lists might yield when you consider your potential. Allow those thoughts to guide you toward the type of work you would love to do, and then see your potential to do exactly that.

After you've asked yourself these pertinent questions, use the following guidelines to temper the steel.

Emotional intelligence. Know your "why." In my case, I'm a difference-maker. I'm a big-picture person, continually improving myself and empowering others. I have integrity and proven business acumen. I have faith. I'm benevolent. What is your emotional intelligence?

Insure your Dream-building against hazards. Understand your challenges and weaknesses. Recognize areas in which you feel insecure and face that insecurity with positive planning. As I read through my past journaling notes, they've revealed that I must choose to overcome my fears to succeed and achieve. Being aware of potential pitfalls has helped me to plan more effectively and to be less fearful of failure.

Listing your potential weaknesses and pondering solutions to your fears, you can completely remove them. Do it with an open mind. What is your biggest fear? What if it happens? How could you fix it? How could you prevent it? I fear failure. I sometimes lose focus. I worry about the lack of resources. But when I face these things rather than run from them, I find them to be false dragons or at least small dragons that are easy to slay.

The most important thing to keep in mind is that we must focus on what we want to see. We must keep our eyes focused on our goals. I remember reading a little article many decades ago about paper tigers, things that look ferocious and scary in the darkness; however, once illuminated—through light and knowledge—and faced with courage, you see that they are painted paper cutouts. Then you're no longer afraid.

"May your choices reflect your hopes, not your fears."
~Nelson Mandella

Step 7: Gratitude

The vital ingredient for Dream-building is a thankful heart. Therefore, when building your dream, you must keep a gratitude journal, making daily notes of things in your life for which you are most thankful—those things, people, circumstances without which your life would be incomplete.

In 2008, following the first stages of burnout and mini-stroke, which significantly affected my cognitive functions for eight years, I consistently worked towards healing, recovery, and retraining. Indeed, I am the phoenix rising from the ashes. Although the healing was not achieved as rapidly as I desired, it did happen; I did heal. I'm now able to complete mind-bending puzzles, something that was previously impossible, even in my 20s.

When I was younger, I believed I had missed out when left brains were issued. I hated complex math, although I enjoy financial math. However, I set my feelings and apprehensions aside for the complex Pathway University Entry Course, completing it in 2017, earning A's each semester, even in the complicated math classes I had dreaded. I'm unsure whether I studied to be employable or to prove to myself or my dear departed mum that I'm as intelligent and capable as any 20-year-old (albeit with much more business and life experience). As you may sense, I needed the Nine-Step Dream-Building Blueprint as much or more than anyone else.

When keeping my gratitude journal, I usually record a minimum of three entries daily, some days, writing several pages. My yearly summary of my 2017 journal is condensed down to this essence of realization, "Significant miracles rise out of seemingly immense struggles." Comparing, I see synchronicities between that journal and the love letter to myself, also written in 2017.

Reflecting on the struggles and the beauty that rose from the ashes of those struggles, I realize what an integral part of creation—a perspective of events and happiness—the practice of daily gratitude brings. The more appreciation I have, the more beautiful things life brings me to be grateful for.

Step 8: Letting Go

I will admit from the start that this might be the hardest but most significant step of all.

While receiving molding experiences and guidance in my life, I comprehend a vision wider and more magnificent than doing everything my way. Learning to go with the flow or swim with the tide, while trying to avoid exhaustion and destruction, taught me to allow and to trust. I'll share how this has manifested in my life.

On November 16, 2015, my much-loved eldest daughter passed suddenly from this life. In the days and weeks that follow, 24 miracles and synchronicities guided me. Here are a few from the earliest days. Even now, it's as if I am present in that time.

As I returned from Sydney by train, I lost phone reception just before the Woy Tunnel. After disembarking, I walk to my car. My shoes are crunching on the gravel underfoot in the car park while I return a missed call. It is a beautiful sunny day. Richard answers the phone and the conversation instantly brings shock and disbelief!

My precious eldest daughter, Naomi, is gone. She has passed over to the other side without warning, no second chance!

Stunned, I cannot even drive the six km home. Stopping at the Gnostic Forest shop, I ask to sit down for a while, trying to think, and sending texts to family, etc., until my friend Jenny can drive the hour or so from Lindfield to be with me. I appreciate my friend so much.

The kind ladies in the Gnostic shop gave me a little dispenser of herbal Rescue Remedy and I immediately pump some under my tongue. It is calming. Mary makes up a beautiful petite rainbow posy of flowers and presents it to me—such bright, joyful, summery colors and divine aroma! So very thoughtful.

Over the next five weeks, amazing miracles follow. I'll share just four.

On Tuesday at 7 a.m., immediately upon waking, I heard Naomi's angelic voice singing "Amazing Grace." It was vividly real as if she is in the room right beside me. Intuitively *I know* this song is for her funeral.

On Wednesday morning, my daughter-in-law, Natalie, wakes to the message she is to prepare a pictorial tribute for the funeral.

On Thursday, I arrived at meditation before 6:45 p.m., 15 minutes early. As I sit in the front row, alone, the music immediately plays: "Amazing Grace," a hauntingly beautiful arrangement by the group Celtic Woman. Never before has there ever been music play before meditation, nor any since. Of all the pieces of music on the track, this particular song played just as I sat down before everyone else arrives.

After everyone is seated, Oscar, the mediator, enters the room, saying that he was directed to select that collection of music. The music playing during meditation has not ever, at any other time included vocals.

My daughters passing away occurred in the early hours of Monday morning. Oscar says her name before I've even had the chance to reveal it. He is telling me many important, intricate details that give me peace and comfort. Naomi relates, via Oscar, that I will not find a suicide note, as she'd had no intention of leaving. Through him, she emphasizes how much she loves me, telling me that I am a good mum and that she does not want me to grieve.

Then, Saturday evening, as I return from Sydney by train, five minutes before disembarking at Woy Woy, a lady who has been sitting behind me approaches saying she has been directed to give me something. She hands me a little white mesh bag containing two lovely crystals, one a smoky quartz with streaks just like Naomi's blond hair running through it. This lady also disembarks at Woy Woy with me, saying she will be in Australia only one week, having traveled from South Africa.

Naomi's funeral has not yet been set. The whole time I am on the train, I have not been teary. Another miracle! Four in five days!

More than 20miracles and synchronicities follow, mostly over the next five weeks.

Suddenly previous disappointment over Naomi taking and selling my black opal and diamond ring a year before melts away, even though I have already forgiven.

This is a truly significant time in my life; learning trust, accepting guidance, and letting go. I know I am powerless to do anything else. Therefore, I'm allowing a broader vision to open up before me.

Step 9: Revision—Reflect, Refine

We have a personal correction system; our own command central, which works on autopilot to help us to revise and refine our reactions to events in our lives. If we allow ourselves to utilize this gift, we avoid wasting years getting to our destinations. Who has time to waste? Certainly not me! I am short of years.

With Step 9, we achieve laser focus and hit our targets effortlessly. We can be our own genies, granting our own wishes and making our dreams come true.

Through this final unusual step, we learn to revise, to reflect, and to reset our goals.

Why is this important?

We are like the autopilot in airplanes, continually correcting the flight path taking us safely to our destinations.

I make a habit of listing my successes at the back of my gratitude diaries. We tend to overestimate our short-term potential and underestimate the long-term. I find that pondering the relationship between constant gratitude, my goals, and the resulting achievements creates magnificent synergy.

When we revise and reflect upon our performances, we can assess our strengths and weaknesses, and discover areas where we require further improvement. Focusing on details, it becomes clear how to refine or reset the next steps to achieve the current goal or to identify new objectives and new goals.

Important observation: Challenges make us stronger by providing valuable learning we otherwise would never know.

We must understand that there is a time and a season for everything. This is exercising and experiencing patience. Patience is so powerful when watching our dreams emerge.

In your journal, list past dreams you have achieved. Then list your current dreams. The listing of recent dreams will show you just how much is possible and how far you've come, thus building passion and power into new dreams.

The cycle begins again, starting with step one. However, there is more momentum now as the foundation has already been established, some steps only requiring revision and small updates.

I have achieved many things in life that I once only dreamed of. I have plenty more dreams to follow. And I will succeed. Watch me create a legacy!

"Every great dream begins with a dreamer.

Always remember, you have within you the strength, the patience, and the passion to reach for the stars to change the world."

~ Harriet Tubman

CHAPTER ELEVEN
From Riches to Rags

By Jennifer Kumer

**"Only those who risk going too far know
how far they can go."**
~ T. S. Eliot

I was born into a wealthy Chinese family and I was
spoiled. When I say spoiled, I mean, I spent $500 on a
haircut and tried to convince my parents that it was normal. It was with that naiveté that I was sent from China
to study in the United States to experience the world. I
attended one of the most expensive boarding schools in
the U.S, where my classmates consisted of second-gen-
eration wealthy kids like me from all over the world. Roy-
al family descents from the UAE arriving in limos and
Asian children with millionaire parents who donated
generously to the school was a norm. Like most of my
peers, I looked forward to which Michelin-star restaurant I was going to dine at on the weekends and which
5-star hotels my friends and I could stay at during spring
break. It was my way of fitting in. A strategy of survival
to hide the pain of low self-esteem and social awkward-
ness I suffered from being bullied earlier in childhood.
I was eventually confronted by the massive gap I had
in my understanding of how the world functioned. The
wealth that I was given so readily and easily as a child
gave me a warped perception of how challenging life

is. Gradually, I became aware that I was a mere product of cultural and social conditioning with desires that were not my own. The more I looked into the mirror of myself, the more confusion there was in personal values and how I truly wanted to live. I began feeling increasingly confronted by the fakeness that surrounded me. "Is this it?" I wondered. Out of my desperation for truth, I started challenging myself, seeking experiences on the opposite spectrum. Instead of luxury travel, I chose to volunteer and teach.

I leaned towards what I was not previously exposed to in my life. I spent a summer caring for orphans and disabled children in Vietnam that had very little. I taught English in schools rebuilt after the earthquake in Sichuan. The gratitude and joy radiating from these children despite their circumstances shook me. It mirrored back my emptiness inside and the shallowness of my desires till then. I was suddenly in touch with the happiness of giving and purpose, an experience no amount of money can buy. The more I experienced it, the more I craved a life of meaning and authenticity. With my longings, I embarked on a quest that would guide me in discovering my truth.

I started to deviate from the life that was expected of me. Instead of attending prestigious universities in big cities like everyone else, I decided to attend an unconventional university that focused on spirituality, holistic living, and alternative education in a meditating community in the middle of nowhere, Iowa. I needed to know who I was and why anything in life mattered. My father sighed and saw my quest as a joke — nothing more than a phase. Throughout my entire university, he only inquired if I had received the money he had transferred and when I planned on taking life seriously again. He never once showed up at my school, nor did he attend my graduation. The more I rebelled from his expectations, the more resistant he became in supporting me financially. Eventually, he made it clear that I'd either have to get my MBA or get back to China not to further his disappointment. I took it as the opportunity to make my declaration. "I am going to live life on my terms whether you support it or not." I chose neither. I abandoned my golden handcuffs in search of a life of freedom. In my stubbornness and pride, I would soon learn the reality of what that means through the school of life.

A Life Of Uncertainty

I've taken two routes in searching for a life of authentic self-expression. The first route was through following my inspiration. The other, which often happens in parallel, is the route of stepping into the dark waters of fears, doubts, and uncertainties. In Jungian psychology, this path is most commonly known as shadow work — the work of befriending and accepting our inner demons. Shame, guilt, envy, jealousy, rage, lust, raw desires, wounds from childhood; these are all shadows kept well-hidden from our awareness that run the show of our decision-making process in an attempt to help us avoid pain. This path is typically the one less traversed because it forces us to confront the distortions of our self-identity, to leave the comfort and familiarity of what we think we know in pursuit of a deeper truth we've yet to uncover. The work of staring into the great void began when I met my twin flame, a man that I love to this day, who came into my life as a mirror to show me the sides of myself that needed love desperately. After graduating from university, every part of me needed a break. In spite of my efforts in proving my worthiness as an overachiever academically and personally, graduating at 20 in both Sustainability and Media & Communications, and being a hardcore vegetarian and 'meditator,' I felt the same confusion on the inside.

I remember a few days after graduation, a loud impulse asked me to Google's ecstatic dance retreat.' The first result that came up was 'Ecstatic Awakening Retreat - eight days of embodied ecstasy and expanded consciousness in the southern mountains of Spain'. Every cell in my body said "yes," and the next thing I knew, I was flying across the world from Beijing on a one-way ticket to this retreat, where I knew no one and had no idea what to expect. This is where I met Bambos, a bald, lean, well-tattooed Cypriot man with mesmerizingly intense eyes. He had an animal-like presence that felt rare, palpable, and raw. He is the kind of man that makes your heart skip a beat without saying a single word. Unabashedly, with his wild, unpredictable and street-smart charm, he commanded the attention of a room as soon as he walked through the door. In the first hour, he walked towards me during an exercise where we had to pair up with a stranger. The activity was simple. Follow your curiosity. One person asks the other questions — anything they want to know without concern of what's "appropriate." Within a matter of minutes of answering his questions, I broke into tears. He sat there, piercing through my masks with his eyes and directness. All of my fears, confusion, and denial came rushing to the surface. I've never felt so naked and vulnerable in front of another human being.

I define twin flame as the person who is the perfect match for you as a result of shared pain. It turns out, despite all of our seemingly polarizing differences in age, culture, and upbringing, Bambos and I shared the same wounding when it came to love. A twin flame relationship is often incredibly intense emotionally. It triggers the feeling of being complete when the two are together. The mirroring nature of the relationship serves to expose one another's inner truths, vulnerabilities, and greatest strengths.

Up until then, I'd been in a pattern of serial monogamous relationships, which all ended with the same pattern of me breaking up with the other, then immediately jumping into the next. I came to the retreat wanting confirmation that perhaps I was polyamorous by nature. Revealing instead was all of the coping mechanisms I've built to hide the wounds of loneliness and unworthiness. I was never able to fully commit and show up fully as myself out of the deep-rooted abandonment fear from childhood. I unconsciously developed the strategy of being the one to leave before I'd be left. Even though I had a "privileged" upbringing, I felt deprived of love and connection. I was sent to boarding school since kindergarten and had learned to shut-down emotionally from an early age. The years of social isolation and being a victim of bullying further instilled my feelings of unworthiness to love. This was the root of my restless romantic life — the reason why I never seemed to be satisfied with enough attention and affection. Deep down, anxiety ran the show by projecting insecurities onto the world around me.

My experience at the retreat suddenly exposed me to a different kind of spirituality. Beyond anything I've ever experienced, it was spiritual in a deeply emotional, intimate, and body-centered way. It was the embodied experience of unconditional love and belonging. I quickly associated my cathartic experiences with Bambos, whom I decided was the fast-track portal towards healing and awakening. We were bound by the hips for the remaining days of the retreat, sharing practices of tantra, authentic relating, circling, breath work, and ecstatic dance. It was exhilarating and confronting at the same time. Whatever this brand-new world was, I felt liberated by it.

All the barriers I've built to suppress and hide my empathic nature felt unnecessary. I could cry, laugh, reconnect with my feelings and express them authentically, allowing others to connect with me. I knew instantly that going back to an old life of numbness was not going to be an option. I was determined not to let go of this aliveness. By the third day of the retreat, I broke up with my boyfriend over the phone. I booked a ticket to Amsterdam, where Bambos lived and based his work as a professional photographer. We lived together in his apartment for a week, celebrating our love with passionate lovemaking and plans of how we can make the relationship work. We both desired to heal our abandonment wounds and move past the old pattern of being the one to leave first. We made a vow that there would be no breaking up from one person's decision. There was to be no break up from tantrum or pushing the other away from reactin. If and when we would separate, it must be a mutual decision made from an emotionally neutral state. We were both excited and terrified by the challenges ahead of us. I decided to be the one to move, so I flew back to the United States to pack up my life. For the next two months, I finished projects, said goodbye to friends, sold my car, and shared my new life direction with my family. The decision seemed sudden and illogical to them; my grand plan was to follow the "love that was calling." But by now, I've built a track record of rebelling against convention that my family gave up on influencing me. I was convinced that I've found the path. The path towards freedom and awakening that I've been longing for since I could remember in the form of a man. I stood by my decision firmly and ignored the opinions of anyone who didn't support my conviction. I was ready to leave my small town behind to start an exhilarating new chapter with my sexy new lover in Europe.

Upon landing in Amsterdam with my life downsized to two suitcases and a heart ready for epic love, the rose-tinted life I dreamed of soon faded and disintegrated before my eyes. I was not prepared to face the crushing weight of my new life. With no friends, no purpose or goals, no sense of belonging apart from my relationship with Bambos, I felt utterly alone. Arriving in the dead of winter, it was dark, wet, and gloomy. I had trouble adjusting to the new lifestyle of cycling everywhere, as I was used to the comfort of driving a car. I had no personal space in the tiny apartment we shared in the city, which was a stark contrast from a house of 15 rooms on a nature trail in Iowa. I became reliant on Bambos for everything, from getting around to laundry-hanging to sharing a bank account. I slowly started losing my sense of independence.

I had no projects to work on as I left my old life behind, so I turned my focus to supporting Bambos photography business to derive a sense of value and purpose. I admired how Bambos built his creative business from scratch and the way he overcame each obstacle that stood in his way. Self-taught in every way, from language to skill sets to building a substantial client base that allows him to travel the world, he realized his dreams by willing and daring to fail. I utilized my skills in graphic design and marketing and soon created a role for myself. Working together added yet another dynamic to the relationship, which soon added complications to our relating. There was a gradual building of codependency, with him on my technical skills, and me on his emotional validation. The more I sought for his validation, the more out of balance our dynamic became. Everything became intermingled, and we started to lose a sense of what we both needed. We triggered and overstepped each other's boundaries often, which would turn into dramas and threats to break-up. But no matter how difficult, we'd eventually find our way back to honoring the vow we made. On the surface, we came back each time, but deep down, we were both becoming aware that it was just an excuse to not think of the more challenging task of facing our own needs. We've become so attached that it became hard to imagine life separately. Our decision to stay together started to stem more from fear rather than from love and respect. The relationship became a place of escape for me, away from the overwhelming dreadfulness of unworthiness, loneliness, and powerlessness.

We attended retreats and workshops together to intervene in our increasingly volatile dynamic. Our life, built upon personal development and shared practices, started to camouflage the toxicity that was building beneath. Symptoms appeared more frequently as we began to feel burned out, emotionally and spiritually. Out of the desire to make space for more lightness, I began attending art classes through Meetup. What was initially just an excuse to leave the house soon turned into an absolute passion. I felt an indescribable relief through the creative process. With each new creation, my desire to express exploded. I began writing, painting, experimenting with whatever medium I could express myself. I followed online courses studying mixed-media art. I lost track of time, regularly creating till past midnight in the living room. It was fascinating to me how my agony, confusion, and overwhelm visually expressed themselves on a page. In the following months, I began taking small courageous steps - sharing my work, attending offline events, making prints and selling at local markets. I started connecting with other artists. I followed my curiosity and spoke to those I admired. The more I explored, the more I was beginning to form a vision of my own creative life. Suddenly, it became apparent that Bambos and I were in different phases of life; he wanted to settle while I was starting to figure out what I want. After a year and a half of living and growing together as a couple, we finally concluded that it was now time to continue our path separately in the name of love. This was a messy process as neither of us wanted to face this truth. In this phase of my life, I learned that following your heart doesn't take you to a set destination. As promised, we parted not from a fight but rather a conscious uncoupling ceremony.

Trusting the Process

"Those who danced were thought to be quite insane by those who could not hear the music."
~ Angela Monet

It didn't take long for us both to see that I was hiding under the shelter of Bambos' creative persona, out of fear in claiming my own. Even though we had invested in turning half of our living room into my art studio, I kept escaping through our collaborations. I kept busy refining his business instead of attending to my own. Doing this, of course, was not sustainable. Resentment built up and eventually manifested itself as tensions and triggers. The ultimate clash came when Bambos gave me the cold hard truth that I was using his business to escape from figuring out my own. The week before we were to present and facilitate at the Mind, Body, Spirit Festival in Cyprus, I admitted that my heart was not entirely with the program. I confessed that secretly, I desired to develop my art project more than anything, but I was afraid of failing. Instead of facing my fear, I put my attention elsewhere. He fell into a silence. Then he announced in a firm voice, "You are not getting on that plane. You'll use this week to figure out the life you truly desire to live. I'll be facilitating at the festival alone, and you'll stop with everything you've been doing related to my business to focus on your work. I don't need you. YOU need you."

My heart sank as I knew this was the last straw sealing the deal. We agreed to each reflect and confirm the details after he returns from his travels. That week became my living hell. With no excuses, distractions, or drama to attend to, all of my fears and anxiety surfaced. I woke up each morning, scared, panicky, and numb. I felt incapable and confused with what I was supposed to do with my life. I fell into a loop of destructive habits - binge-eating, binge-watching and not leaving the house. I filled every minute with things to do. I kept myself glued to the computer. I felt ashamed of my thoughts and couldn't bring myself to any form of social interaction. I'd watch the sunrise and set in my pajamas, festering in self-pity and blame. I couldn't breathe deeply. I couldn't create, write, or sit still with my mind. I couldn't imagine a life without the safe harbor of my relationship. Who would I be without the person that transformed me into who I am? I felt paralyzed in my decision making and unable to step out of my triggers and story. Without my previous financial comfort, I realized I had very little confidence in surviving on my own. I didn't trust myself to take care of myself in many ways. The impending end of my relationship only mirrored back all of these existential anxieties. On the final days of locking myself at home, I had a panic attack. In my trembling hysteria, I knew I needed help desperately. After some research, I dialed up several mental health clinics. I was informed that I needed a special note from my general practitioner. I didn't have one at the time. After more searching, I discovered the limited options I had and the long wait for appointments. 'This is not going to work,' I thought to myself. As I sat in my emotional paralysis and ticking deadline, I felt the slow but sure deterioration of my psyche. I dialed the emergency line. "I feel suicidal, depressed, and emotionally unstable. I need help." I was booked for an appointment the next morning. Sitting in front of a tall, gray-haired Dutch doctor, I spilled my tears and struggles. I wanted his note and his confirmation that, indeed, I was depressed so that maybe I could make sense of my overwhelm. "You're experiencing the symptoms of depression because you're going through a lot and feel alone. You need community, family, friends, and social support more than anything right now. I'll give you this note, but know that therapists are not going to solve your problems." I half-heartedly nodded and took his note. I called the mental health clinic, immediately forwarding the note and asked for the quote and the next available appointment. I was shocked to find out that intake alone was going to be 700 euros, and depending on the treatment plan, the estimate could be anywhere from 3,000 to 9,000 euros, not covered by insurance. It was a truly confronting moment, as apparently, I was too broke to be depressed. Even if I did invest in getting help, it wasn't going to sort my life out automatically. I suddenly understood the doctor's words. I knew that the financial burden would create a setback for me personally and professionally. I still had no clue where I was going to live and how I was going to kickstart my business. It got me thinking, what if I invested the same effort in my dreams? How far could I get if I gave myself the financial, emotional and professional support I need to manifest the life I want to own? In fact, what are the existing resources that I can utilize? Something clicked in me. The answers were suddenly right in front of me. All the communities I've been a part of were just a Facebook group away. I was part of an online, intimate active sisterhood group called Deep Inner Knowing, with women from all over the world committed to the embodiment of creativity, and authentic living. I asked for help openly and vulnerably. First, through writing, then through live videos. I live-streamed as I curled on the kitchen floor sobbing. For five minutes straight, I muttered the same words, "I'm so scared." As I bared my heart, love poured in. I started receiving regular phone calls from various women from the group. The calls became my lifeline for the following weeks, jumping on calls, crying and releasing, receiving encouragement and affirmations. Some told me their own stories, some sang for me, some brought transmissions of love, some cuddled with me sharing silence across the screen. I remember cracking up when one of the sisters, an ex-military single mom with two kids, said to me with a serious face, "Oh honey, I feel you. I've have had PTSD and depression like a motherfucker since 2015." We both chuckled and had a good laugh. Gradually, I regained a connection to my inner feelings and started sharing my art project, the Empathic Wisdom Cards; a card deck illustrated by me, portraying the full spectrum of emotions accompanied by a guidebook with games & practices designed to help people connect with their feelings. This was a gift I wish I received as a child and the tool I desperately need as an adult. People were excited and the words spread. With the encouraging momentum, I launched it as a project on Kickstarter. It was an emotional rollercoaster as I had to move out during the first week of my campaign. I had an all-or-nothing deadline to make. As I kept busy preparing for the launch of the project, I was also dealing with the heartbreaking reality of separating with the man that I loved while searching for a new home in a foreign country and packing up my old home. I had to sleep on the couch because being in the same bed was too painful. There was hardly time to process the immensity of this transition emotionally. I shared with him my desire and intention to bring closure to what we shared through a conscious uncoupling ceremony. We asked the small group from the 15-month training we joined as a couple to support us. The last training weekend happened right before I had to move out. It was an extraordinary experience to be held by the group who've witnessed every stage of our relationship. It was a true gift to be seen in the chaos and beauty of what we've shared. We were asked to leave the room while the group reorganized the setting for a ritual they had created for us. When we came back in, the room had chairs in two rows facing each other, forming an aisle, much like a wedding reception. We were each asked to pick someone from the group who would accompany us as we walked towards a big flipchart in the middle of the room. There was a line drawn right down the middle with two markers on each side. We were asked to fill up our side of the paper with what we love about the other. The room witnessed us as we each scribbled away. "Relentlessly determined." "Courage." "Passionate expression." It didn't take long for my page to fill up. When we were both finished, the ceremony leader, our shared mentor, passed me a pair of scissors. I was told to cut till halfway and then pass it to my ex, who will finish cutting the other half. We then folded each other's half and held it before our hearts.

"Exchange your pieces of paper, return the projections of what you love about the other back to yourself. From this point on, you'll carry those parts of the other within yourself." The words reverberated in our hearts. The room cried with us as we exchanged the paper.

Days later, with the help of a friend and a moving van, I packed up my life once again and left. I had a Kickstarter goal to reach and a deadline to make. The Kickstarter project that would launch my career. To this day, it is the proudest thing I've ever created that is a direct transmission of inspiration. The card deck became the only thing I lived and breathed. In the attempt to save cost and simplify my life, I moved to a tiny anti-squat room far out of the city that had no floors, fridge and wifi. I invested in a business coach with the money I saved and began implementing structures and routines.

I went to the library each day to work, spent time regularly in nature, doing yoga, journaling, dancing, and connecting with friends. I learned to hold myself accountable, to show up and to keep myself disciplined physically and emotionally. I learned that accountability could be an act of self-love when balanced with compassion towards one's self. I learned that there are days where getting out of bed is enough of an accomplishment and others where you need to sit yourself before the desk and do the work lovingly. I decided that the best way to move on from the relationship was to embody all the qualities Bambos inspired in me. I overcame my fear of rejection by becoming vocal in sharing my creative ambitions. I pitched to venues to host events, offered online workshops, and took every opportunity I had to share the exciting creative baby I was birthing. I took actions to realize the fantasies I would previously dismiss. I started trusting my instinct more. I visited countless art studios and co-working spaces for rent. In old factory buildings and artist collectives, I discovered the concept of artist residencies where, for a set duration of time, artists lived and worked on a specific project, then had some form of presentation to show their creations, usually in the way of an exhibition or performance. As soon as I learned about it, I knew I needed that; a space to explore, create, and experiment as an artist. I applied to every matching opportunity I could find online. I trained myself to have a positive outlook when met with limitations. For the first time since moving to this country in a year and a half, I finally started exploring and appreciating it — the nature, culture, freedom of self-expression, awareness in health and spirituality. I started falling in love with being where I was. Soon, the universe heeded my call and aligned for me to be at the right place at the right time, to talk to the right person. I landed a three-month artist residency in the best neighborhood in Amsterdam near Vondelpark.

I was chosen as a last-minute applicant and offered a gorgeous two-storey studio with a kitchen and bathroom for a nominal price, and gallery support for a solo exhibition. More opportunities soon opened up. Strangers from all over the world were interested in the card deck and emails of gratitude for my work came in regularly. By popular demand, the solo exhibition expanded into a workshop, and the workshop became part of a creative retreat program. Facilitators from other modalities began using the cards in their work at festivals. The cards are now at my favorite store in Amsterdam and I coach several clients in their creative processes. I have a few artist residencies already lined up. I never could've imagined being where I am had I not trusted the leaps of faith one step at a time.

Here I am, six months later. I left the man of my dreams, financial security and my comfortable home to find myself. If there is one thing that this journey has taught me, it is that I'm no longer rushing towards a destination. I'm already living my most aligned reality in each moment. I am in the perfect place at the ideal time, and wonderful things are coming to me. I've put in the hard work of healing and now I get to harvest the fruit of joy. I know I'll look back years from now at my 23-year-old self, who was starting to get it, and I'll love her for living and sharing her life audaciously, despite her fears. I have learned one of life's greatest lessons, and I am almost certain that it'll not be the last time I learn it. It is in standing in our fears that we learn to shine. Acting in the moment of our greatest weakness is our greatest strength. When we dare to embrace our humanness, beauty and magic happen.

"Create your own life."

~Unknown

Author Biographies

John Spender

Chapter One

John Spender is a 17-time International Best Selling co-author, who didn't learn how to read and write at a basic level until he was ten years old. He has since traveled the world, started many businesses leading him to create the best-selling book series *A Journey Of Riches*. He is an Award Winning International Speaker and Movie Maker.

John was an international NLP trainer and has coached thousands of people from various backgrounds through all sorts of challenges. From the borderline homeless to very wealthy individuals, he has helped many people to get in touch with their truth to create a life on their terms.

John's search for answers to living a fulfilling life has taken him to work with Native American Indians in the Hills of San Diego, the forests of Madagascar, swimming with humpback whales in Tonga, exploring the Okavango Delta of Botswana and the Great Wall of China. He's traveled from Chile to Slovakia, Hungary to the Solomon Islands, the mountains of Italy and the streets of Mexico.

Everywhere his journey has taken him, John has discovered a hunger among people to find a new way to live, with a yearning for freedom of expression. His belief that everyone has a book in them was born.

He is now a writing coach having worked with more than a 170 authors from 34 different countries and his publishing house, Motion Media International has published 20 non-fiction titles to date.

He also co-wrote and produced the movie documentary *Adversity* starring Jack Canfield, Rev. Micheal Bernard Beckwith, Dr. John Demartini and many more, coming soon in 2020. Moreover, you can bet there will be a best-selling book to follow!

Dr. Colleen Sabol-Olitsky

Chapter Two

As a partner in a world-class dental office for 15 years, Dr. Colleen Olitsky has always had a passion for helping and serving others.

A lover of exercise and self-care, Colleen has learned so much over the last decade about nutrition and how to achieve optimal health while aging gracefully.

These passions have ignited a fire in her to assist others in improving not only their physical health but also their financial health and mindset. Colleen believes that she has discovered the vehicle to achieve all of that and more.

Dr. Olitsky enjoys spending time at the beach, reading, traveling, and writing. She is the author of The Naked Tooth: What Cosmetic Dentists Don't Want You to Know.

She is married to her best friend, Dr. Jason Olitsky, and together, they reside in Ponte Vedra Beach, FL, with their children, Chase and Gabriella.

Tony Gunn

Chapter Three

Tony Gunn is a business owner, world traveler, musician, engineer, author, and healer. Coming from an under-privileged home in rustic America, he knows what it's like to start with a dream and then materialize alternate realities.

As an Alchemist and traveler, Tony has redefined what it means to transcend all information with love. As an engineer, Tony has helped implement successful strategies with some of the largest companies around the world. As an author and musician, Tony has provided inspiration, connection, and authenticity to people of all backgrounds.

These days, you can catch him at one of his symposiums or simply laying in a hammock, lost in nature, between realities.

Lyn Croker

Chapter Four

Life coach, speaker, writer, mother, and founder of Superwoman vs Realwoman.
Life is like a roller coaster with lots of ups and downs, fears, doubts, and challenges.

Having been a paramedic, Lyn understands human behaviour and what makes us "tick." She researched and travelled the World learning about people for over 30 years.

Lyn has experienced and overcome many of the challenges life throws at us from childhood trauma, PTSD, depression, being in a wheelchair, obesity, raising four children while juggling a demanding career, divorce, and a child abusing drugs and alcohol.

We all need a helping hand; someone who understands you and what you're going through.
Her 4-step program:

1. Helps you develop a success mindset to achieve all your dreams and goals.
2. Gives you clarity about what you want.
3. Enables you to uncover your self-sabotaging habits and blocks that are holding you back.
4. Gives you the confidence to make changes in your life.

With these simple tools, you can overcome challenges quickly and easily, and achieve what you truly want.

Change Your Thinking, Change Your Life

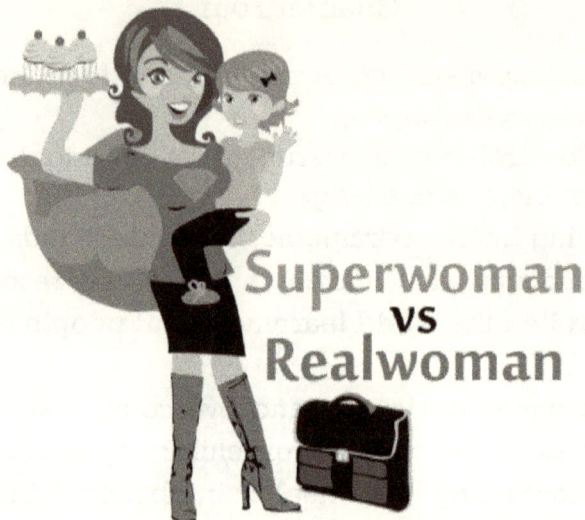

www.superwomanvsrealwoman.com

Ph:0402 254 042

Email: lje196@gmail.com

Beth Lydia Ranchez

Chapter Five

Lilibeth Ranchez Villegas was born and raised in Antonio, Delfin Albano, Isabela, the northern part of the Philippines, preferrably called Beth.

The eldest of five kids of the late Jaime Ranchez, Senior and Iluminada Macadangdang Ranchez.

Graduated in High School as a Valedictorian with two Gold medals and a granted scholarship by the University of the Philippines but chose Far Eastern University where she was also awarded a full scholarship. She graduated with a Bachelor of Arts major in Economics Degree. She was aTop Notcher of the National College Entrance Examination (NCEE).

Beth joined the Philippine Armed Forces in the Philippines as a Civilian employee and migrated to Australia in October of 1986. She studied Financial Planning and worked for the two big banks in Australia.

Proud mother of Cristina Ashliegh who also follows her mum's profession in the Financial Planning Industry, and Blake who is currently completing his double Degree in Computer Systems Engineering and Computer Science Engineering.

Dario Cucci

Chapter Six

Dario works with businesses to show them how to increase sales through building better relationships with their customers. Companies often waste thousands of pounds trying to find new customers, only to lose them in the first 12 months with poor customer care.

Keeping a customer happy and loyal is much less costly than finding a new one and Dario teaches a simple and practical approach to building lifelong loyalty and long-term sales.

Dario first learned how to sell in his twenties when he made his living from 100% commission-based selling with Anthony Robbins Events. Over the following 15 years, he developed his own Relationship Sales System that teaches you how to build relationships that lead to sales and long-term loyalty.

Visit his website to get in touch with him to book a call on Skype

www.dariocucci.com

Leon Beaton

Chapter Seven

Leon is a life/spiritual coach who empowers his clients to take control of their life. He assists people to see the bigger picture of their life from the perspective of their soul. Utilizing his psychic abilities, NLP, Reiki, crystals, sound and Oracle cards, Leon has developed a unique healing technique to assist people in releasing the pain of the past, find clarity in the present and enable them to embrace the future, whatever it may be for them.

Leon's work has expanded to working more with men who are struggling with the changing expectations and 'definition' of what it means to be male.
Leon's work has taken him to many parts of the country of Australia and around the world.

Leon is a combination of compassion and forthrightness in assisting people in embracing the changes in the new world.

Contact Leon, leon@leonbeaton.com, to find out more about his work.

Lynette Gehrmann

Chapter Eight

Lynette (Angel Knight) is an Intuitive Energy Medicine Practitioner and Transformation Teacher. In writing, Lynette channels a higher perspective.

Combining intuition and logic, Lynette can read and translate the unconscious/subconscious of her clients. This has led her to want to share her insights through writing.

To Lynette, her work is a lifestyle, continually uplifting and inspiring, and often healing deep-rooted emotional pain and stumbling blocks in a simple conversation.

'The smile of relief on a person's face is everything to me, every time,' she says.

Lynette's healing of trauma and spiritual awakening has, over the past 13 years, completely changed the direction of her life. Dreaming a whole new life into being has been the result.

To contact Lynette, visit: www.AngelKnightAuthor.com

Cindy Vazquez

Chapter Nine

Cindy was born from immigrant parents who were born in Mexico. She was raised to follow her dreams and work hard for what she wanted in life. Gifted with the opportunity to be born in the land of the free was a huge blessing.

To honor her parents, Cindy pursued goals to become a college graduate and embrace her career in interior design. Her journey was of becoming that successful woman while fulfilling the current opportunities of being a military wife, and a mother.

Becoming a mother, a wife and a military wife has granted me the awareness of being grateful for the lessons throughout the years I have moved and travel to different states within the USA. These opportunities have provided me with the patience to become a better version of myself and continue to pursue the dream while I can help others do the same.

Narelle Burgess

Chapter Ten

Narelle is the eldest child of (hard) working-class parents from Sydney. Missing School numerous times due to Bronchial Asthma; she somehow made it to Year 10, School-Certificate.

Three years later, she got married and was then blessed with five children. She now has 15 grandchildren.

Out of necessity, she helped to create, develop and run two family businesses, as well as two of her own. She sold three for significant profit.

Age 39, Narelle served as financial Planner for 14 years with a major organization, which was rated No 1 nationally for five consecutive years.

Her working relentlessly during GFC resulted in burnout/mini-stroke, thereby losing significant cognitive function and a lifetime of financial assets, business, home, and investment properties.

In 2009, Narelle became a hypnotist. She was performing healing while retraining (10 years) in Life and Business Coaching, Property renovation and development.

Coach, Speaker and Presenter, Author, NLP Master-Practitioner/Trainer, Hypnotist.

With passions in Property Refurb/Renovation and Development.

Phone 1300 16 37 47or Email narelle.burgess@ymail.com torequestyour **free copy of any/all**

* The "9 Step Dream-Builder Blueprint" workbook
* 1 Free Coaching or Healing Session
* 1 Free Strategy Session
* Preview 1st Chapter of Narelle's next six books

Jennifer Kumer

Chapter Eleven

Jennifer Kumer is a self-taught visual artist, design activist, self-publisher, and trained creativity coach devoted to helping 'empaths' heal and thrive through embodying their full creative potential.

Originally from Hong Kong, she received her education in the U.S and later on moved to Amsterdam. Jennifer now lives a semi-nomadic lifestyle, traveling and creating artist residencies while coaching and giving talks and workshops based on the Empathic Wisdom Cards. She is passionate about creating social change through art, emotional education and personal development.

Find out more at www.jenniferkumer.com

"If you want to achieve greatness stop asking for permission."

~ Unknown

Afterword

I hope you enjoyed the collection of heartfelt stories, wisdom and vulnerability shared. Storytelling is the oldest form of communication, and I hope you feel inspired to take a step toward living a fulfilling life. Feel free to contact any of the authors in this book or the other books in this series.

The proceeds of this book will go to the Bali Street Kids Project, in Denpasar, Bali. The project gives orphaned and abandoned children home, meals and education. You can donate to this fantastic cause here: https://ykpa.org/.

Other books in the series are...

Liberate your Struggles : A Journey of Riches, Book Eighteen
https://www.amazon.com/dp/1925919099

In Search of Happiness : A Journey of Riches, Book Seventeen
https://www.amazon.com/dp/B07R8HMP3K

Tapping into Courage : A Journey of Riches, Book Sixteen
https://www.amazon.com/dp/B07NDCY1KY

The Power Healing : A Journey of Riches, Book Fifteen
https://www.amazon.com/dp/B07LGRJQ2S

The Way of the Entrepreneur: A Journey Of Riches, Book Fourteen
https://www.amazon.com/dp/B07KNHYR8V

Discovering Love and Gratitude: A Journey Of Riches, Book Thirteen
https://www.amazon.com/dp/B07H23Q6D1

Transformational Change: A Journey Of Riches, Book Twelve
https://www.amazon.com/dp/B07FYHMQRS

Finding Inspiration: A Journey Of Riches, Book Eleven
https://www.amazon.com/dp/B07F1LS1ZW

Building your Life from Rock Bottom: A Journey Of Riches, Book Ten
https://www.amazon.com/dp/B07CZK155Z

Transformation Calling: A Journey Of Riches, Book Nine
https://www.amazon.com/dp/B07BWQY9FB

Letting Go and Embracing the New: A Journey Of Riches, Book Eight
https://www.amazon.com/dp/B079ZKT2C2

Making Empowering Choices: A Journey Of Riches, Book Seven
https://www.amazon.com/Making-Empowering-Choices-Journey-Riches-ebook/dp/B078JXMK5V

The Benefit of Challenge: A Journey Of Riches, Book Six
https://www.amazon.com/dp/B0778S2VBD

Personal Changes: A Journey Of Riches, Book Five
https://www.amazon.com/dp/B075WCQM4N

Dealing with Changes in Life: A Journey Of Riches, Book Four
https://www.amazon.com/dp/B0716RDKK7

Making Changes: A Journey Of Riches, Book Three
https://www.amazon.com/dp/B01MYWNI5A

The Gift In Challenge: A Journey Of Riches, Book Two
https://www.amazon.com/dp/B01GBEML4G

From Darkness into the Light: A Journey Of Riches, Book One
https://www.amazon.com/dp/B018QMPHJW

Thank you to all the authors that have shared aspects of their lives in the hope that it will inspire others to live a bigger version of themselves. I heard a great saying from Jim Rohan, "You can't complain and feel grateful at the same time." At any given moment we have a choice to either feel like a victim of life, or be connected and grateful for it. I hope this book helps you to feel grateful, and go after your dreams.